RECKLESS GRACE

RECKLESS GRACE

A Journey to Freedom from Shame, Brokenness, & Lies

Whitney Roehl

AUTHOR'S NOTE: While the details about my family and my life experiences are true and accurate as best as I can remember, I have taken slight liberties with the timeline. Also, the character of Grace (as well as her mother and boyfriend), her experiences, and my interactions with her are a work of fiction. Writing about my life was challenging in many ways, and creating a young female character with whom I could interact not only helped me process my life but also helped me write and shape this book.

CONTENT WARNING: This book contains references to attempted suicide, generational sin, and alcoholism.

Dedication

I dedicate this book to two very important men in my life:

My amazing husband and life teammate, Jake Roehl. I love you.

My dad, Timothy Joeckel, who served our country at the young age of twenty. We'll see each other again in Heaven.

Ranger, Warrior, Hero, My Dad

Only six months in the army you became a Ranger.
200 men volunteered with ruthless day and night training.
There's a better chance of surviving with Ranger men, you
    reasoned.

You were one of six who passed.
The commanding officer said, *You follow what Joeckel does and
    you'll live.*
Forty-nine kills with a five-man team on your very first
    mission.
You were trained to turn into an animal.
It was *kill or be killed,*
And you were mad at God for it…the brutal fighting of men.
Rangers Lead The Way, they say.

You turned twenty-one in the 115-degree fields of Vietnam,
    but you didn't tell anyone.
Being on the injured reserve didn't keep you from going on
    missions.
A Bronze Star, the third highest medal you can get, you
    received and many more, with honors.

I want to live the life of danger as a Ranger, your team sang as
    you ran day and night carrying forty pounds on your
    back.
Not even a wild panther stood a chance—you killed it in two
    jabs after it attacked you in the jungle.
By seventy-one you forgave your enemies.
You loved God. Jesus was your friend and Savior.
But now, Ranger, Warrior, Hero, Dad, you're free from all
    this pain.
I can't imagine the sacrifice you made for our country.
I'm grateful for your service.

You taught me to be brave, resilient, and believe in myself.
You taught me to trust God with every area of life.
You taught me to have joy and not worry.
You taught me to stand up for what's right, to take risks,
    and dream big.
But most importantly, you taught me to marry a good man
    who loves Jesus.

Dad, I wouldn't be who I am without you.
I'll miss Maverick getting to know you, but he'll learn about
    your legacy.
I love you.

CONTENTS

Preface

It took me six years to write this book. For several years, each time I sat down to write, a new traumatic memory or shame from my past would taunt me. God put it on my heart to write this book as a testimony; in hindsight, I can see it was an invitation to do a deeper level of healing.

I felt God put this book on my heart because I see many Jesus followers who avoid sharing their "skeletons in the closet." There's a religious spirit condemning each of us as a church body. "Well, at least I'm not as bad as she is," we say, pointing the finger. "I can't share that struggle or people will reject me" is a shared fear. I want to be an advocate for more grace, love, and acceptance while we go through our struggles, not just after we've conquered them.

I feel the Lord wants more transparency and honesty from our lives, instead of us giving each other the "put together" version of ourselves. No, it's not comfortable to share so vulnerably, but I believe true healing begins when we bring these stories and memories to the light, His light. Jesus doesn't condemn you or me. It's a big fat lie that we must "fix ourselves" before we are accepted at church, although I hear often that has been people's experience.

My prayer is that this book will be an example of a bold, painfully raw honesty that will bring you hope in your circumstances. I'm kind of laughing, but I'm also very serious.

I want you to see how broken, shame filled, and hopeless I was because it's the truth. I have zero interest in sugarcoating my experiences because there was very little sugar. It was like taking a straight shot of cheap whiskey—it stung from the moment it hit your lips and stung all the way down your throat.

My prayer is that these pages will plant seeds for a new level of faith and that the Holy Spirit begins a supernatural deeper work for an inner freedom and renewal of your mind. My prayer is that your heart will soften, your broken places will be healed, the eyes of your heart will be awakened, new life will be breathed into your bones, and your spirit will be encouraged for fresh hope. Most importantly, I pray you feel the Father's love like never before, freeing you from all anxiety, unworthiness, shame, and anything that's not His will for you, which is always good. I believe, my friend, you are reading this book at the perfect time, and it's by His grace that you will get exactly what you need. I bless you in Jesus's name. Amen.

Acknowledgments

First, I want to thank my talented husband, Jake, for helping me craft my memories and lessons into a book in a beautiful way, creating the cover, believing in me, being supportive as I healed by writing this, and parenting so I could get away to write. You truly are my God's best. I love you, Handsome.

Thank you, Patty Yandell, for walking me through a deeper healing process six years ago that set me on this amazing adventure with Holy Spirit. Thanks for being my spiritual mom with unconditional love.

I want to thank the Osterhoudt family for always being my safe haven growing up. May God bless you like you've blessed me.

Last but not least at all, thank you, Nathaniel Hansen, my editor who patiently walked me through this messy process of turning my thoughts into a book. You are a gift from God to help make this dream come into a reality.

CHAPTER ONE

God's Transforming Work

I SAT IN A CUTE, beachy café, sipping a hot cup of black coffee while I waited for Grace. It was a chilly morning, the doors were open at the café, and I could feel my toes already going numb but loved the fresh-smelling ocean breeze. I was looking forward to my time with her, and this café was one of our favorites.

Grace was a beautiful but fiery young woman. She had freckles all over her face, red hair with blonde highlights from being in the sun so much, and light hazel eyes. She was about my height, five foot six, with an athletic build. Like me, she was very active, loved to surf, backpack, play beach volleyball and anything outdoors. We had first met at church in our small beach town. Grace rarely missed a Sunday because she was dating a guy at the time whose dad was an elder.

We had started meeting for coffee every week because she was going through some rough patches. At that time, I was her youth leader, and she was a sophomore. Now she was about eight months from graduating from high school. I couldn't believe time had gone so fast the past few years.

Grace snuck up and wrapped her arms around me for a big hug.

"Aww, there you are," I said, enjoying her affection. She wasn't always this warm toward me. Over the years of us meeting she'd become much more comfortable expressing her admiration, which I enjoyed experiencing. Grace had a big heart deep down, but it took getting past a lot of internal guards and self-protection she'd built up. I could completely relate though. It's what made our relationship so unique and strong. Grace and I understood each other in ways many people didn't.

"You smell like you just got out of the shower, fresh and sweet," I said.

Grace came from a rough family; her dad left her mom and siblings for another woman when she was nine. She was the oldest of six kids with a lot of responsibilities. Her mom was a functioning alcoholic who struggled with depression and extreme social anxiety. Grace had a lot of pent-up anger but hardly ever expressed how hurt she really was. Over the years of getting to know her, I could see how painful it still was from her dad leaving them and how difficult her home life was.

"Yeah, I decided to shower for you today. You're the only person worth doing it for." Grace sat in a chair across from me, glancing at the floor.

We sat in the coffee shop for the next hour, and I listened to her latest gossip of friends, guys, and how home life was going. I genuinely enjoyed hearing her perspective on life. She'd done so much growing over the last year especially, and I loved seeing the woman she was becoming, although at times it seemed like she was taking one step forward and three steps back. Our conversations were never surface level. We both loved to talk about our faith and get down to the meat of what was really going on in life. We were both big thinkers, often getting lost in our heads instead of being present in the moment.

The server came by to top our coffee off, and Grace never even looked up. I smiled at the young lady, apologizing with my eyes.

"Whit, my mom's such an idiot. Have you ever felt like…like, you couldn't care less if you never saw your mom again? Like you're just so frustrated with her that you think life would be better if you never talked?" Grace asked with genuine curiosity and a note of sadness.

"To be honest, yes, but not with my mom—it was with my dad." I never wanted to sugarcoat things with Grace, and as she'd matured over the years, I'd gotten more honest about my past when she asked questions because I knew she was becoming mature enough to handle it.

One of the many things I loved about her was how inquisitive she was, especially for her young age. She wanted to hear stories so she could relate and learn from them. Grace hadn't always listened to me with such honor and curiosity, but over the years, as our relationship grew, she became one of the best listeners I know.

"Whit, you never talk about your dad. What was your relationship with him like?" Grace leaned in toward me over the coffee table. "I mean, most of our conversations are about faith, or I'm doing most of the talking." She smiled and sipped her coffee.

"That's the way I prefer it though—you doing most of the sharing. I'm an open book. You know I'll share anything with you." I laughed nervously. I genuinely didn't mind talking about my family or my past, but it still wasn't super easy to reflect on and talk about, even after all these years. I'd preferred to not bring it up. I figured that since Grace was almost in college, it was a good time to be more open about the transformation God has done in my life. I'd always share powerful testimonies of God's love, redemption, and healing but didn't into depth about my personal pain that preceded.

"Well, my relationship with my dad was...full of disappointments. That's probably the best way I'd explain it."

"Sounds familiar." Grace rolled her eyes.

"I was in second grade when my parents split up. I remember the day my mom told me that she and my dad were getting a divorce. It was a huge relief, and I was definitely more grateful than sad, but it was for good reasons.

"My dad had severe PTSD from serving in the Vietnam War, and the way he dealt with it was drinking. I can honestly understand his choice—he was only eighteen when he was drafted. I couldn't imagine being that young and being forced to go into hand-to-hand combat. From the beginning, he decided to train to become a Ranger because he knew being surrounded with the most elite men was his best chance of surviving his time in war. He was right.

"Growing up I had no idea that an Army Ranger was an elite-level person who became a lethal weapon who went on special close-combat missions. At your age, he trained to become an animal, so he could survive. He was one of twelve other men who went on missions no one else would know about. To this day, when I go to the VA clinic with him, people who hear his story honor him right there, saluting him. My dad was a big deal in the army, but to me he was just my dad.

"Anyway, I tell you that, Grace, because before I share a story, I don't want you to have a bad opinion about him. He's an honorable man who gave his life for our country and suffered for the rest of his life," I said, tears welling up in my eyes.

"Okay. I'll do my best to not be biased," Grace said, smiling slightly.

"Thanks. It'd been almost a year of my parents living apart. My older sister Brooke was a senior, so she was gone a lot. It was up to me to help Mom with my sister Sunny and my brother Chance, but I didn't mind. I was grateful we didn't have to deal with my dad's drinking and unpredictable behavior every day.

"The only bummer about them splitting was when it was Dad's weekend to have us. I dreaded those weekends. I never knew which version of him we'd get. It was rare that he stayed sober even though he was court ordered to stay sober when we visited. My stomach was always in a knot on those weekends. I tried to maintain a good attitude, but it was hard when my anxiety was high, and I'd feel extremely irritable. I wanted so badly to enjoy weekends with him, to have great memories, but it almost never happened. It was hard to put my guard down. I had to consistently be on alert to protect myself and my siblings. I'd done it all my life, and as a ten-year-old girl, I was the one who always got help or called the cops when Brooke wasn't home. Plus, I felt fully responsible for Sunny and Chance when we stayed with him. It was my job to protect them from disappointment and harm. It felt like a heavy weight, but I didn't know anything different.

"That afternoon I said a quiet prayer, 'God, please keep us safe and help my dad not to drink this weekend. Thanks.' Then the three of us kissed Mom goodbye and got in Dad's light blue Chevy truck to ride thirty miles to his apartment, in another town. I hated being so far from safety without knowing many adults who could help. There was one guy, Randy, who lived on the first floor. He was friends with my dad and knew how my dad would get when he drank. He had told me on a few occasions, 'You let me know if your dad gets a bit crazy. I know how he can get, so don't hesitate comin' on over. Okay, young lady?' I'd nod my head, but didn't feel completely safe going to Randy, unsure if he would side with me or my dad when it came to it.

"I'd looked for signs of him drinking since we got in the car. I'd already checked under the back seat if he was hiding beer or a pint of whiskey, paying close attention to see if he was slurring. There were no signs. *Whit, just relax, you're so negative and uptight,* I thought. I was quiet the entire drive while Chance asked Dad question after question. He was in first grade with a lot of personality. Chance looked up to my dad with eyes of awe and wonder. I hated how much he loved my dad because of the amount of constant confusion and disappointment he experienced. Somehow, he never lost hope in my dad like I did. I guess being four years older, I was more aware of what was going on, where we tried to hide as much from him to protect him as best we could. When we arrived at Dad's two-bedroom apartment, my stomach was still in knots.

"'Let's make spaghetti and watch a movie tonight,' Dad suggested, seemingly excited about our plan for the evening, but he'd forgotten to go to the grocery store before coming to get us. 'I'll be right back. I'm gonna run to the store to grab dinner to make and Oreos for dessert. You guys can watch *Saved by the Bell* while I'm out. Whitney, you're in charge.' When he shut the door behind him, it was about 5:30, and I was already really hungry.

"Once I heard his truck leave the parking lot, I opened all the cabinets, checked under his bed, and checked the closets. I was pleasantly surprised—no alcohol.

"*Seriously relax, Whitney. You're so uptight. Why can't you just trust Dad that he won't drink and wants to spend quality time with us?* I thought, forcing myself to sit back on the couch to watch TV and enjoy time with Sunny and Chance. I hated feeling on guard all the time, but I'd been wrong before when I'd thought things were going to stay calm. Those nights, I had a hard time forgiving myself, replaying the scene in my mind over and over, obsessing on what I should have done differently or how I should have spotted the danger sooner. Afterward, I literally wouldn't be able to sleep for nights, and I'd have reoccurring nightmares. Sometimes I'd make myself physically sick, and I'd miss school because the worry and anxiety overtook my body.

"Two hours had passed. Still no sign of Dad. I wondered if he'd gotten into an accident. Chance and Sunny kept asking where he was because they were starving. There wasn't much food in his cabinets. He was clearly living a bachelor life, going out for all his meals. I didn't have a cell phone, so I continued to distract them with TV. Then around nine o'clock I heard keys opening the apartment front door. As he walked in, my relief turned to terror.

"I could always tell when he'd been drinking. His big thick glasses were halfway down his nose, the Rangers hat he wore all the time was tilted up and to the side, and his Wrangler jeans sagged off his skinny waste. My dad was six foot four, a tall but slender man with a small beer belly. I always thought he was a handsome man, but in moments like this I saw him as a different man. He was no longer my dad—he was an enemy to be feared.

"'Where were you?' I asked hoping he'd be honest about the drinking I knew he'd done while he was out.

"He came in with a brown grocery bag, swaying a bit to the side. His eyes locked on me, as if I'd just insulted him.

"My throat felt tight with fear and rage, and my stomach was nauseated with devastation. There was no telling what would happen. I needed a strategy, but I also needed to assess how bad the situation really was by listening to the number of words he would slur and how much he staggered. I'd be able to tell from the level of his intoxication whether I needed to get my brother and sister to safety or if we'd have until morning when I'd call Mom to pick us up a day early.

"It didn't take longer than five minutes to know he was bad, he'd drunk a lot, and I needed to get us out as soon as possible. My biggest challenge was not to let him know I was planning to escape, or else things would quickly escalate. That'd happened several times before. It didn't matter how drunk he was—he knew I was the one plotting and planning on a way to escape. 'Don't be trying any of your ridiculous ninja moves. I know what you're doing, Whitney,' he'd say, slurring his words. I hated that he remembered I was the one who'd get us to safety but didn't care because I felt a purpose of protecting Chance and Sunny.

"'It's none of your damn business where I was. I'm the adult, and you're the child,' my dad slurred as he stumbled into the kitchen and slammed the grocery bag onto the stove. His apartment was small, but it felt even smaller when he drank. There wasn't much room to hide or go privately so I could call Mom.

"'I'm sorry. I was just worried. I'll get the noodles started then I'm going to use the restroom, okay?' I said, trying to keep calm. I emptied the bag of groceries—a twelve-pack of Budweiser, Oreos, and pasta noodles. I knew he'd gone to a bar to drink because he no longer cared about hiding his alcohol. He'd forgotten the hamburger meat and sauce for the pasta, but I knew we wouldn't be eating anyway. I'd be happy if we made it out safely without one of us getting beaten for no reason, but I had no clue how we would actually get out.

"My heart raced even more, and I wondered if I was going to vomit. My palms were sweaty as my mind replayed the other times when things had gone horribly, but at least with those, we had been at home so we could run to our neighbors, the Osterhoudts, who were like a second family to us.

"'Stay calm, Whit,' I said quietly. I snuck into the bathroom that was attached to his bedroom, grabbed the cordless phone, and quietly called Mom. 'You've got to come get us. Dad's drunk. You've got to hurry—it's bad,' I said without explaining any of the details.

"'What the hell are you doing? Calling your mom and trying to get me in trouble?' My dad yelled from outside the bathroom.

"I hung up, unsure if she'd trust me enough to be on the way. I had to figure a way out myself.

"'Who the hell do you think you are?' he bellowed.

"I took a deep breath, trying to calm myself. The calmer I stayed, the better chance I had of keeping him calm. That wasn't always a guarantee, and sometimes it backfired. 'Dad, I'm sorry, I was just calling Mom to tell her *goodnight.*'

"'You liar. Do you know who I am? I'm a Ranger licensed to kill, and I could kill you in seconds, just like that.' He punched his palm in the air.

"His king-size bed was between us. I needed to make it over the bed somehow and out the door without him grabbing me. He'd reached the point of no return—I saw it in his eyes. There was a rage that appeared, and he was in Ranger mode, which was when things always got out of hand, usually ending with the cops rescuing us and taking him to jail. Anyone who wasn't an officer who tried to intervene would also be in danger. He had lethal skills. I'd seen him fight with strangers, and it was scary watching him do things I never thought he'd actually do. There was no time to waste.

"'Dad, I'm sorry,' I said. 'Can we just have dinner and watch a movie?' I still hoped to calm him, so I could come up with a plan.

"'I have killed more men than you want to know, little girl, and I can kill you. Look at this uniform.' He turned around to point at his army uniform hanging up in his closet behind him. That's when I jumped across the bed, barely swiping past him as he turned around to grab me. My legs felt like Jell-O as I sprinted for the front door. I heard him stumbling toward me as my hands shook, and I fumbled with the door lock just in time to swing it open. I ran to the stairs, grabbed the railings, and jumped the entire flight of six stairs. All I could hear were his cowboy boots, but I couldn't tell how close he was behind me. I didn't want to look back to check, so I continued to jump every flight of stairs until I reached the first floor. I banged on Randy's apartment, assuming he was sleeping and wouldn't hear me. As I banged desperately on his door, screaming for help, I tried to think of my backup plan.

"My dad yelled from upstairs, 'I'm your father. You get back here!'

"I hated when he reminded me that he was my dad. It gave me a twinge of shame, like I was being a bad girl, disobedient for getting help. I'd heard it enough times though that I knew I couldn't trust that part of me. I reminded myself that he was no longer my dad in these moments.

"Randy swung the door open, and I fell into his arms, sobbing hysterically. 'Help! Sunny and Chance are still up there. Save them, please.' I hated that I'd left them up there. He called the cops as I crawled behind his couch, afraid my dad would come down, break in, and hurt me. I sobbed hysterically, rocking back and forth. 'How could I be so stupid to believe he'd stay sober? I'm so stupid. I left them upstairs. I'm stupid, stupid,' I said, still shaking and unable to calm myself.

"The cops arrived shortly after. When they did, I was still in a fetal position, trying to stop shaking and crying. The image of him yelling 'I could kill you!' replayed in my mind over and over. The guilt of leaving my brother and sister behind was thick and heavy. It seemed too much to bear. I wanted to die—the emotions were so intense. I doubted that my body would ever feel safe and calm again. Even though these unpredictable events happened regularly, I'd never heard my dad talk about killing me. A new level of fear was branded in my mind.

"It wasn't until one in the morning when Mom and Brooke arrived to take us home. I was grateful Mom had taken my call seriously, and I was relieved to see Brooke, who had a way of making me feel safe.

"The cops said they found my brother and sister hiding under the bed. After all that, somehow my brother didn't want to leave Dad or understand why we couldn't stay with him for the weekend. It angered me to see him upset because he didn't understand what had just happened.

"'Chance, stop crying! Can't you see how unsafe it is to stay with Dad?' I shouted as Brooke comforted him. I had forgotten how young he was and expected him to be more aware of the danger we were in. He'd suffered the consequences of Dad's drinking a handful of times, sometimes being whipped with branches until he bled. Yet, somehow, he still had an unbreakable love and hope that Dad wouldn't act that way.

"My emotions still felt so dark and heavy like they could put me in a coma at any moment or that I'd just faint. I felt crippled from the intense guilt and hatred toward my dad for not staying sober and from my frustration for thinking that this time could have been different.

"The red and blue lights flashed as I got into the back of my mom's car. The cops were upstairs talking with Dad in his apartment as we drove away. I didn't know if he'd go to jail that night, but honestly, I didn't care. I was exhausted, and I was sick of being let down that he'd stay sober. It was hopeless. I didn't want to care about him anymore. Honestly, I would be fine if I never saw him again.

"As I crawled into bed at home, my adrenaline pumping but body exhausted, I prayed, 'God, thanks for getting us home safely. Please help us not to have to go back to Dad's ever again.' And after that I fell asleep."

I sighed and looked from the window of the café back to Grace. Her mouth was slightly open, speechless. I'd forgotten where I was.

"In a snapshot, that was my childhood. I could write a book about it except I don't remember my childhood outside the traumatic memories like that. It's mostly black though when I think back, not remembering much. Everything feels foggy, like a dream." I laughed, trying to lighten the heaviness.

"Wow. That's intense, Whit. It's incredible you are where you are in life. If that were me, I'd probably be addicted to drugs just so I wouldn't have to feel that pain," she said with sternness.

I laughed. "I've said that many times. If it weren't for experiencing Jesus's love, redemption, and healing in my life, I would be totally broken and hopeless. Thankfully, Jesus has transformed me from the inside out. I carried around a lot of unworthiness, shame, and brokenness from my childhood that I believed was just part of who I was. I believed I was permanently broken. Now, I know it was a lie. I used to think God must not love me because he gave me that life, but my life is one big testimony of God's faithfulness. In the past, sharing this story would be triggering, but it's not anymore. In my journey, I've learned powerful tools as a coach to renew my mind and make the changes I craved. Jesus did the deeper work that would have taken me decades, and He did it in years, sometimes months. I still have more growing to do, but I'm grateful for the transformations I've had."

I paused, remembering that the previous week, while traveling from Tucson, Arizona, I had a nightmare that woke me up, sobbing as I reminded myself it was just a dream, even though it felt so real. "Unfortunately, even today, I'm still having nightmares from time to time where I'm running for my life from my dad and feeling tremendous guilt for not saving Chance and Sunny. It's wild how real those dreams feel, like I'm transported back into my childhood. I'll usually wake up sobbing, but within thirty minutes or so, I can fall back asleep peacefully. Thankfully, I don't have them as regularly as I used to, and I still believe I'll be completely released from them some day," I said calmly before sipping my very cold coffee.

"My dad's basically dead to me for leaving us, but if I were you, I would actually hate my dad," Grace snapped.

I thought about the anger I'd had toward my dad and God. It haunted me how I didn't want anything to do with either of them for years.

"I can understand that. I spent many years wanting nothing to do with my dad. I was angry, like the raging anger that feels so deep you think it's just a part of your personality, not knowing that what you actually need is healing. Since most of the memories I have up until I was fourteen are traumatic, I felt justified harboring my anger, like my anger was what would keep me safe from the deep disappointment I'd feel when my dad would drink again. Eventually, I realized that anger and unforgiveness were preventing me from the healing work Jesus wanted to do. Once my eyes were open to the harm it was causing me, I forgave my dad, completely. It was one of the harder things I've done. I can genuinely say forgiving him was incredibly freeing, like it closed a door I was leaving open to the devil to influence my mind and life. The relief and healing I've experienced through that forgiveness journey, with the help of Jesus, softened my hardened heart, freed me from bitterness, and made me more compassionate toward my dad's struggles. I now see my dad actually did love his family even though he was hurting from PTSD. That journey of forgiveness led me to healing, freedom, and now a lifestyle to instantly forgive others or myself. It's a habit that keeps me walking in freedom."

I didn't want to pressure Grace into forgiving her mom for the hurt she experienced, but I wanted to be honest about the power of forgiveness. I could tell she was discouraged with not wanting to forgive her mom.

"Well, I'm sorry to say I haven't reached that place of wanting to forgive and not sure if I ever will." She looked down, fidgeting with her jewelry.

"That's okay, Grace, just keep bringing it to Jesus. He's the One who helped me get to a place of willingness. He's the author and perfecter of us and our faith." I paused, thinking about what it was that really transitioned me from anger to forgiveness.

Grace had a blank look on her face, like she was feeling guilty for not being able to forgive yet. She had always been hard on herself, very self-critical and had little to no compassion toward herself when she struggled.

"Do you want to know what made a big difference in helping me move toward forgiveness without feeling pressured or justifying what happened?" I was ready to hear an honest "no" if she wasn't interested. She was always upfront—it was one of the things I admired about her. She was straightforward and did little people pleasing.

"Sure. On one hand, I like being angry because it feels powerful, but on the other hand, I hate the way it constantly consumes my mind," Grace confessed, taking a big sigh with tears welling up in her eyes.

"That is the truth—holding onto past hurts takes up a ton of mental real estate. You have great self-awareness, Grace. What helped me make a big leap toward forgiveness was renewing my mind—the way I saw myself, God, and life. I got serious about making it a daily practice to exchange lies—those hopeless, fearful, or shame-filled thoughts—for God's truth. When I didn't, the sneaky lies would seem factual and keep me living in the prison of harmful emotions and behaviors. I had to train myself on who God says I am, not what my past says I am. For example, I remember believing three painful lies that felt factual at the time: 'I'm broken beyond repair, I'm not worthy of love, and if people really knew my past, they'd never be friends with me.' Those lies kept me feeling powerless, broken, and isolated. No matter how much time had passed, those overwhelming negative emotions were there to torment me. Finally, when I learned how to write down the lies and cast them off in Jesus's name, then to practice declaring the truths that I am fully loved by God and worthy to receive blessings, I have a purpose and future that's as bright as the sun, and I am powerful and authoritative in Christ, it changed the way I saw myself, which changed the way I experienced life. That's when my desire to forgive became stronger, and eventually I let go of my past hurts through a forgiveness prayer between God and me about my dad and past trauma. That forgiveness started me on a radical journey into greater freedom. I felt lighter, more hopeful, and bit by bit transformed to the person I am today. If I hadn't started to change the way I thought about myself first though, I think I'd still be carrying that heavy burden. I'd be stuck and full of pain."

Grace looked at me, then dropped her head, gazing at the floor like she was defeated.

I looked at her compassionately, wanting to just give her a huge hug. "Grace, are those lies resonating?"

"One of them definitely does: 'I'm not worthy of love,' and I'll add to that, 'I can never trust anyone again.' Well, until you came along, Whit. Other than that, I don't trust people. I feel like I have to protect myself from disappointment, and I don't feel good enough, like I'm a failure even though I've had success in school. I feel like I always come up short, needing to prove my worth or something, but I didn't know I was believing those lies until now." Grace wiped a tear.

"That's really great self-awareness," I said, smiling at her, awed by her courage to see the hard truths but knowing how healing it could be for her.

"Whit, you're seriously the only person who gets me. I can be myself without feeling like you judge me harshly, but you steer me in the right direction. Like a role model—yeah, you're the role model I never knew I needed. I'm really grateful God brought you in my life." She glanced down, rubbed her hands on her pants.

"Total side note, but can I ask you a personal question?" Grace said with a change in tone, as though she was getting more serious than our already very serious conversation.

"Always," I said, smiling with curiosity.

"Do you want to be a mom someday? I don't mean to ask if that's a tough subject. I've always wondered over the years. Now, seeing the impact you've had on my life I just had to ask." Grace's compassion and thoughtfulness warmed my heart. I hadn't seen her be this considerate toward others— even me—that often.

"You can ask me anything, Grace, and that's a great question. As of right now, no. Jesus has done a lot of inner healing in me, but being a mom isn't something I can trust myself to do yet. I still worry I'd be neglectful or dysfunctional in ways if I had kids of my own. For right now, I'll just stick to mentoring, so I don't mess someone up too bad." I was making light of a topic that was very heavy on my heart that I rarely brought up. The desire to be a mom had grown more and more over the last year, but I didn't see how it would be possible. I'd spent quite a bit of time talking to Jesus about it, but I had a lot of mixed emotions.

"That makes sense. Okay, last serious question; then I've gotta head out. Did you ever shut God out, ya know, like push Him away for what He allowed to happen to you?" Grace asked.

I pondered her question, trying to recall examples to give her an honest answer.

"Goodness, you came with all the right questions today," I said genuinely impressed with her insight. It felt connecting to have Grace asking me such in-depth questions, like she really loved me.

"Hmmm…yeah, I guess I did. At some point I stopped believing He was good and only saw Him as the one to blame. A big part of my anger was toward God. I couldn't believe that He really loved me since He let those horrible things happen. If He were really good and worth trusting, then surely He would have interfered and stopped so many bad things from happening to my siblings and me. Those thoughts stirred up a lot of doubt in Him and left my heart bitter from my teenage years and into my twenties," I answered.

"Thankfully, He pursued me, even when I was angry at Him. Now, after I've learned more about who He is, and my knowledge of Him has grown, I don't blame Him at all. I know He didn't cause or allow those things to happen. Every person has free will. But even with people having free will, He promises us—His children through Jesus—to make all bad things work together for our good. My life is full of evidence of His promise. I can honestly say He's healed my past trauma on a level I didn't think was possible and turned my sorrow into strength. For example, I am resilient—my faith is strong like an oak tree whose roots run deep. I have a peace that goes beyond human logic, so I'm able to stand steadfast when life gets crazy. I own two businesses, which God knew I desired. Thanks, God! My life is literally one testimony after another of His goodness and blessings overflowing. Someday, Grace, I will write a book about it all so I can share the power of Jesus's love and our Heavenly Father's reckless grace. Now, I see the emotional and physical pain I experienced as being a greater reward. Even this moment, sharing all this with you, is part of my God-given purpose from that pain. None of that would be possible if I hadn't gone through the healing process with Jesus and the journey of renewing my mind so I could learn to think in possibilities of my future and getting rid of the old feelings of hopeless from my past. Anyway, I could go on and on, but those are a few ways God helped me stop running away from Him and start running toward Him. I'm truly forever changed because of His overwhelming goodness." I could tell Grace wasn't fully convinced with my answer, but I trusted I was planting seeds in her and trusting that God would do the deeper work.

"Yeah, I don't know if those type of blessings are worth all that." She laughed.

"I've gotten you to trust me, Miss. I won't trust anyone ever again," I said jokingly. "That wisdom you refer to didn't come from a pain-free, easy life, ya know?"

A young girl out the window caught my eye. She must not have been older than seven, with knots in her hair and some raggedy clothes. I wondered where her parents were and if she felt loved. My heart grew heavy for this little girl outside. Immediately, I was thrown into a flashback . . .

I peeked my head in my mom's dark bedroom—she was still in bed with another migraine.

"Mom, I'm going to church, then youth group after. I'll be home later this afternoon," I said softly but loud enough to make sure she heard me. The covers were pulled over her head, with a bowl beside her bed. That's when I knew her head hurt really bad—she often got

sick from the pain. Sometimes, it ended with me calling the ambulance to take her to the hospital for a shot.

The house smelled like stale alcohol from a party she had the night before.

This was a typical weekend morning, not always resulting with her having a migraine but at least sleeping until late morning. I hated being home on Sundays because the house was dark. There was the smog of cigarette smoke, the house messy with empty cans and bottles. It felt depressing, and I hated that my mom spent most of the day irritable from not feeling well and sleeping it off.

"Okay, Sweet Pea. Make sure your brother and sister get lunch, and please clean up everything when you get home. Love you," she said, slightly poking her head out from the covers.

I had daily cleaning chores, but on the weekends, it was my job to clean up the mess from their parties. I didn't mind because I couldn't stand the house staying dirty like that. It made me feel better to clean it as soon as I got home. The hardest part was our laundry room in the old scary basement. It constantly had piles of clothes and towels, no matter how many loads I did. When my friends were outside shooting hoops or playing basketball games at the park, I still had laundry to do.

I was just thankful for the nearby Methodist church, only a few blocks away. It was a safe place, and I looked forward to going every Sunday morning and to going every Wednesday night for youth group. I liked the youth pastor, Mr. Johnson. He was also my math teacher since I was in eighth grade. He and his wife were like mentors to me. They treated me like a kid of their own ever since I started attending church regularly about two years earlier. Now that he was my math teacher, our relationship was even closer.

"Hey, Whit, great to see you this morning," Mr. Johnson said as I walked in the room. I felt a physical relief whenever I saw his smiling face. His wife usually took their three kids to their Sunday school while he taught our Bible study. I was the first to arrive, and

it was just Mr. Johnson and me in the room waiting for everyone else.

"How was your weekend? Is everything okay at home?" He asked with a sincere curiosity.

Mr. and Mrs. Johnson were aware of my parents' separation and the drinking that went on at home. Plus, I babysat for them once or twice a month, and afterward I'd stay and talk with them a bit. They both made me feel so loved, supported, and always made me laugh when things got too heavy. Plus, I admired their marriage. From my point of view, he and his wife loved each other very much, and I hoped to have a marriage like theirs someday. Mr. Johnson was in love with his wife—you could tell every time she walked in the room. It was so unfamiliar to me that sometimes I felt unworthy in their presence. They seemed normal, and I wasn't, but I was grateful anytime I got to be around them. Mr. Johnson could tell my shyness was a feeling of unworthiness and would encourage me.

"Whitney, you're smart, beautiful, and talented. Don't think anything different about yourself, you hear me?" he'd say sternly.

When I heard those words, they fell dormant. They didn't feel true. "I came from a broken family, so that made me broken," I'd think but I'd agree, "yes, sir," hoping to change the subject.

"It was all right. My mom has a migraine again. I feel bad for leaving her alone, but I had to get out of the house. Sunny and Chance are still sleeping, so I could leave without having to drag them along." I smiled, trying to avoid my heavy anxiety.

"I'm sorry, Whit, but I'm glad you're here. How's your journaling to Jesus going? Is that still helping you feel more peaceful at night?" he asked, grabbing his Bible out of his briefcase and putting it on the table.

He and his wife had suggested writing out my worries, fears, and anxieties to get them out of my head and onto paper. They said to end my writing with a prayer or a scripture verse. That's exactly what I'd been doing for the last three months, and it was helping me feel more hopeful about my family.

"Yeah, I've been doing it almost every night. Can I share one with you? I brought it because I like to use this journal for taking notes, too," I said, excitedly unzipping my backpack. I enjoyed sharing with Mr. and Mrs. Johnson because they reminded me of Brooke: fun and loving people I admired.

"Of course, I'd love it. If other people walk in, then just pause and you can finish after class," he said, putting his hands on the table and giving me his full attention.

"Okay, sounds good. I wrote this one two nights ago."

Dear Jesus, I've heard you can do the impossible, so I'm going to ask you to do a miracle in my family. My dad just got out of a thirty-day rehab. I was really believing he'd be cured—no longer wanting to drink and staying sober. On his way home from rehab he ended up drinking again. I was really angry and ran away, wanting to give up on believing he'll ever get healed. The disappointment, Jesus, is just so painful, but Mr. and Mrs. Johnson encourage me to keep trusting You. So this is me trying to trust You, even when it feels hopeless and scary. Will you please help my dad stop desiring to drink and help me to keep trusting You in the day to day? My mom struggles taking care of us kids all by herself, and I feel overwhelmed trying to help all the time. I want to play with my friends but feel guilty when I do. Will you help me to be a better daughter and sister? Thanks, God, for listening. Love, Whitney.

Mr. Johnson had tears in his eyes, and for the first time I saw him show emotion. "I'm sorry, Whitney. I didn't realize your dad had gotten out of rehab and went back to drinking. That's hard." He looked down at his hands that were in a prayer position, paused, then looked back up at me.

"It's important to me that I tell you this, so hear me out. You are not your parents' choices. What they choose to do or not to do doesn't make you any less lovable. Whitney, you're made in God's *image with a God-given, glorious plan and a uniqueness that this world needs. I don't want you to see your parents' actions as a reflection of you being less worthy or loved. You have a Heavenly Dad, through Jesus, who is your Provider, Protector, and He is the One who will take care of you. I know Jesus is going to work powerfully through your life, Whitney. Anyway, I'll get off my soap box, but I wanted to be sure you heard that. Please let me know if you or your siblings need anything. Our home is always open to you."*

I could tell he was trying to be supportive and not make me feel uncomfortable. It took everything inside of me to not run over to hug him and ask him to adopt me. CPS (Child Protective Services) had been called on different occasions, but no one actually made any changes for us. We were always stuck with the aftermath of my mom being embarrassed and my dad being outraged that people weren't minding their own business.

My hope was dwindling that things would improve. Plus, I was physically exhausted from putting on an act to teachers and friends that I was handling the responsibility of Chance, Sunny, school, helping my mom with chores and cooking, and dealing with my dad's drunken episodes. Sometimes I felt like I could just sleep for days, being so exhausted, hopeless, and frustrated that it was overwhelming.

Instead, I smiled at Mr. Johnson, then another student walked in the room and sat down across from me. Both Mr. Johnson and I looked at each other with a "we'll talk later" look then changed the topic.

I was just grateful for people like Mr. and Mrs. Johnson who encouraged and loved me. They gave me a safe place to come on Sundays and took me in like a daughter of theirs by checking in with me throughout the week. My relationship with Jesus felt stronger than it ever had from the time I started going to church on my own. I loved youth group and the friendly church community. Learning about the Bible was making more sense to me than it had in previous years. Writing to Jesus at night had become a habit and helped me go to bed with a lighter feeling.

*   *   *

Two years of my parents being split up I began living in an unfamiliar joy and peace. Those moments were new. I was excelling in basketball, playing trumpet, getting As and Bs, and having a blast with friends. I felt connected, loved, and more supported than I'd been used to experiencing.

It was weird though. Even with all of the good going on, I'd still have waves of fear. My friends still teased me, from time to time, "Just relax, Whit. You're always worried." I tried to hide my anxiety of wondering whether my mom, Sunny, or Chance were safe at home while I was gone with friends. I'd remind myself, "Dad is thirty minutes away in Cozad—you're safe."

It was the end of my eighth-grade school year, my favorite year so far, when I finally felt like the hope in my life had grown so big that nothing could crush it. I had been dating the most popular guy in our school, Heath, for several months. He drove a red 1969 Mustang. Athletic and respectful, he made me feel so special. As I walked home from the last week of middle school, I couldn't help but skip with excitement about the awesome summer my friends and I were going to have, the summer before we transitioned to high school together. We'd been talking about this moment for years—how we we're going to win championships in sports and how they'd be some of the best years of our lives.

As I approached home, I spotted my dad's blue Chevy truck in our driveway. This was a rare sight. "What's going on? Is it Dad's weekend? No, it's Mom's weekend," I reassured myself.

I'd already made plans to stay at a friend's house the next day. My stomach tightened up, my heart raced, and I jogged to the house, feeling fear and urgency wash over me.

"Something bad must be going on," I thought, worried Mom or my siblings were in danger.

"Honey, we're in the dining room," my mom yelled when I entered.

I walked in to see Sunny, Chance, Mom, and Dad all sitting at the table.

"What's going on? Why is Dad here?" I blurted. I didn't like the way this looked.

"Sweetheart, we have exciting news for you. Your daddy and I are getting back together, and we're moving to Colorado," Mom said, looking over at my dad and smiling.

I felt like someone just punched me in the stomach, taking my breath away. Adrenaline pumped through my entire body. Fearing what I might say or do, I turned around and ran out the door. I had no idea where I was running, but I had to leave—I couldn't stay in that dark house.

"Whitney Lee," I heard my dad yell as he pushed his chair back.

I was already out the front door in a dead sprint, hysterically crying. My worst nightmare had just come true. I'd soon be trapped in a new place—no safety net of people I could run to—with the man I despised and feared.

I didn't know where I was running, but I had enough anger fueling me that I could sprint for hours. As I sprinted and cried past every house, I wondered if they saw me, but I didn't care. All my hope for a better future was gone. The dim light at the end of my tunnel was now shut off. It was black. I reached our park where I'd spent countless nights playing basketball with friends until the town curfew horn blew. It was a place I felt safe—I knew everyone who came to the park.

I stopped, still crying, now trying to catch my breath, fell to my knees, and pounded the ground. "God, where are you?" I screamed. My heart was beating so fast, my face was hot, and my head hurt from all the crying.

"You've completely abandoned me. I've been seeking you, going to church regularly but You're nowhere to be found. Why are you hiding from me?" I prayed inwardly as anger pulsed through my

veins. My mind swirled with ideas of how I could escape this death
sentence: moving to a new place, new school, but worst of all with
the man who I'd experienced disappointment and danger from more
times than I could count.

"God, when my dad drinks again and becomes dangerous, who
will I run to? I won't know anyone. I hate you, God, I wish I never
pursued You. It's a lie that you love me. Mr. Johnson lied to me—
You're not a good God," I said inwardly. I rubbed tears and snot off
my face and then got off the ground.

"Whit, it's time to toughen up. I have to stop trusting people like
Mr. and Mrs. Johnson who gave me false hope. I've gotta stop caring
about people, so moving will be easy. I'm stupid for letting people
get close to me. That's why I'm in this horrible situation," I thought
as I felt my heart numb. Suddenly I felt more powerful as the anger
grew, and my heart hurt less.

The new idea of closing off my heart was now my new hope. I'd
figured out how I'd handle the fear and sadness of my move. I'd cut
off all my love for the people I grew up with. They couldn't matter
to me anymore because it was painful and not worth it. The pain
had become too unbearable, and the God I'd put my hope in no
longer was worth trusting. Now, it was up to me to protect myself
from the pain. I had to toughen up and stop allowing myself to be
hurt by others.

I had a new vision of my future. Gone was the old vision of my
dad getting sober and my high school years being spent with friends.
As I allowed the anger to stir, I felt more determined to never let
anyone get close again. Closing my heart off to the people I loved
there was necessary. I had to stop caring about them because it'd be
too hard to let myself love them like I do while living in another state.
I thought that it was stupid of me to trust people the way I had since
no one really cared about me. If they had cared, I thought, I wouldn't
be moving. Someone or God would have rescued me because they
knew my situation. As I considered all that, the anger intensified,
and I was more motivated to push people and God away.

"Do you hear me, God? I said I hate you!" I shouted to be sure there was no confusion that I wouldn't be pursuing Him anymore. It felt powerful to say out loud, with just a subtle uneasiness in my stomach, like I was doing something wrong and getting away with it. I knew it was a risk to push myself away from God and the people I loved, but it was a risk I was willing to take. My decision was made. I went back home compliant.

That night when I went up to my bedroom, I grabbed a stack of my journals from under my bed, tearing page after page out, lighting them on fire, and flushing them down the toilet. "I'll no longer be writing to Jesus," I thought.

"Whit! Hello, Whit," Grace said, waving her hands in front of my face.

"Oh, sorry, Grace. I got distracted by that little girl outside." I went to point out the window at the little girl with raggedy hair. "Well, she *was* there." I didn't want Grace to know I was distracted by more childhood memories. I got frustrated with how often my mind would see random things and drift off into a flashback; it felt like a trance came over me. I'd be transported back to random memories with zero control over it, but I didn't know how to prevent it from happening. "At least the flashbacks didn't carry as much heaviness as they did five years earlier," I thought.

I walked away from our coffee time grateful for Grace's and my relationship because on one hand I was able to use my pain for a greater purpose by sharing my experiences, but on the other hand, it was healing to recall some memories without feeling shame or guilt.

*   *   *

That anger toward God, from that young age of fourteen, was the beginning of a self-protective pattern I continued to use for years, into my mid-thirties. Have you ever had trauma or a life event that takes you to such a dark pit, that you questioned if you'll be able to bear the pain, so you do your best to numb your heart? Maybe you do it by pushing people or God away with fear or anger. Ultimately, you feel hopeless, and the idea of the future being better is dead. It's a painful place to be.

For me, numbing my heart with anger and keeping people at a far distance was the only way I could think of that would prevent more pain from happening. In hindsight, I know it's a pattern of childhood trauma to self-protect. I've finally reached a place of healing where I've learned tools like how to be more self-compassionate instead of shutting down with anger. When I look back on this moment where my life felt like it came crashing down, I no longer have shame for getting angry at God. Shame or condemnation is never from God. Now, I know God was grieving with me. He didn't cause my parents to get back together, and He hadn't forsaken me. He was right there with me, and even while I threw my fists at Him and cursed Him, He was loving me with compassion and understanding. Over the years, I've encountered His Fatherly love countless times—to the point of inner transformations that can't ever be taken away.

It's the same for you. Whatever you've gone through or are currently going through—childhood trauma, a death of a loved one, divorce, poverty, cancer—it doesn't matter how hopeless or dark it is. There is hope because of His goodness and love for you. God has never left your side and never will. You may have emotional or physical healing to go through, like I did. That's okay. Jesus wants to walk hand-in-hand with you to take your burdens, your wounds, and exchange them for wholeness from His supernatural healing. Jesus wept with you. He knows what it means to suffer emotionally and physically. He has unlimited amounts of compassion because He also suffered—to the point of death on a Cross.

CONSIDER THIS

Then Jesus said, "Come to me, all of you who are weary and carry heavy burdens, and I will give you rest. Take my yoke upon you. Let me teach you because, I am humble and gentle at heart, and you will find rest of your souls. For my yoke is easy to bear, and the burden I give you is light." (Matt. 11:28–30)

We all have hard events that happen to us, and no one goes through life with perfect parents or a harm-free experience. From these disappointments or hardships we can easily carry regret, resentment, or bitterness. I carried my childhood trauma and disappointments around like heavy luggage for years without knowing it. At age thirteen, my burdens tainted the way I saw God. He seemed distant, cold, and neglectful — similar to my earthly dad. My perspective of God and myself grew darker as my burdens became heavier. I had little to no belief that there was much good in either of us. These lies became strongholds like cement walls that felt impossible to break down. This was the area that God wanted to set me free from, heal, and transform for my good and His glory — in my mind, spirit, and heart. Nothing is too hard, overwhelming, dark, or impossible for God. He wants *you* to go to Him, so He can begin this beautiful process.

What heavy burdens are you carrying? A burden can be an event or relationship for which you no longer have an optimistic expectation, and you feel obligated to keep holding on to it. Maybe you're holding on for self-protection or you don't feel worthy to release it, and you've gotten so used to carrying it that it's become a part of the way you see yourself. That's okay. We all have seasons where we're tricked or unaware of the burdens keeping us from entering our promised land.

Often, these burdens manifest themselves as negative emotions like anger, apathy, shame, guilt, unforgiveness, or bitterness. When you spot these feelings that reoccur in your life, it's an invitation for you to face them and invite Jesus into that process. They're like a "check engine" light that comes on in your car. It's easier to acknowledge when you decide to drop the self-judgment that you're having them. Nothing's wrong with you—all humans experience difficult circumstances that cause uncomfortable emotions. It's what you choose to do with them that makes the difference. It'll either grow your character or keep you running from them in self-destructive ways. I've seen the denial and self-destruction in my own life and lives of many others.

Here's an exercise to open the door to a new level of freedom. Ask the Holy Spirit, "Am I carrying any heavy burdens that you want me to let go of?" Just pause and write down whatever first comes to mind—don't overthink it. This is a powerful exercise I've used that's grown my relationship with Jesus and allowed me to have faster revelation than any other practical, self-help tool out there. The Holy Spirit knows you better than you know yourself. He is a safe, loving, and gentle Person who wants you to experience more of your Heavenly Father's love. It will require you to invite the Holy Spirit into these secret places and to learn how to listen to His voice, trust Him, and follow through.

I invite you to say this simple prayer:

Heavenly Father, thank You for the awareness of these heavy burdens I've been carrying. Forgive me for holding on to them with hopelessness or bitterness. I'm sorry for trusting in myself or others for the answer instead of You. Today, I give You these burdens. They're not mine to carry because Jesus already paid the price for all my pain and heavy burdens. In Jesus's name, I release [share what heavy burdens you're handing over], and I refuse to pick them back up. I receive Your peace, comfort, easy yolk, and healing today, Jesus. Holy Spirit, come now and do the deeper work and finish what I began by faith. Amen.

CHAPTER TWO

It's Not Working

G RACE BOLTED IN MY FRONT door, sobbing, and ran over to the couch and put her head in her hands.

"What's wrong?" I walked over to her, put my hand on her back, and sat willing to be next to her as long as she needed.

She looked up, mascara running down her face. "I'm an idiot, Whit. I'm so stupid. I did it again," Grace said with guilt and shame all over her face. She didn't have to say much more—I knew what she was referring to. When we met, she'd confessed about the drinking she started when she was thirteen to help her cope with anxiety. That choice led to her being sexual with multiple guys, and her friends at the time were doing it too. When we started meeting regularly, she'd decided to stop drinking and messing around.

"I'm sorry, Grace," I said, conflicted on what else to say. I didn't want to rush her processing her emotions. Feeling the heaviness she was carrying, I prayed inwardly, "God, give Grace comfort right now and let her feel Your unconditional love through me. Take off all shame and guilt; that's not from You. In Jesus's name, Amen."

"Why! Why do I keep doing this? I'm stupid, stupid, stupid!" Grace's anger flooded to the surface as she sobbed more.

A memory flashed through my mind from my high school years. I felt a wave of shame cover me, then peace, almost like a gentle reminder of the relatability I had with Grace. I knew the emotional pain from shame could feel so real that you didn't know how to get out from underneath it. I felt God nudging me to share.

"Can I share something I haven't wanted to tell you until now?" I wanted to know if she was ready to hear it or if she just needed to vent.

"Sure," Grace mumbled, wiping the mascara from underneath her eyes.

Nervousness rose inside me, making me afraid to tell her this part of my past because I didn't want to taint how she saw me. Then I reminded myself that my vulnerability was to give her hope and know she wasn't alone in her struggle.

"When I was in high school, like you, I was very popular. Every year, except my freshman year, I was voted homecoming queen. You know I felt a lot of external pressure because so many people knew me and liked me, but inside I was full of anxiety. Well, my junior year, to challenge my popularity I decided to date a rebellious guy, James, a star athlete at our school. I thought that maybe if I dated the bad boy, I wouldn't be so popular and not have all this pressure. Silly reasoning, I know.

"Well, six months into our very passionate and fun relationship we started to fight about his jealousy of me talking to guy friends. Eventually, our fights turned into heated arguments in the parking lot. James would tell me I was worthless, stupid, or an over-dramatic baby. I felt so disrespected and hurt. I'd respond by getting physical; then it ended with me driving off. One day, I felt so angry, I texted Ryan, whom I'd had a crush on for years. Not wanting James to find out, I secretly met up with Ryan and well…" I said, my face warm and stomach in a knot, not wanting to say the words.

"We had sex. I'd love to say that was the first and last time, but it wasn't. It went on for about four or five months. I'd be with James and then sneak off to be with Ryan. I was constantly going back and forth. In the moment, I felt powerful and invincible, but after I felt small and full of shame. I wanted to break up with James, but when we were good, it was so fun. I wanted to end things with Ryan, but he was so sweet, and I could tell he cared so much about me. I'd tell myself, 'Okay, today is the day you break it off,' and I'd try but we'd end up working it out. Eventually, my heart just grew cold—I didn't care about hurting either of them. Then one day, James caught Ryan and me making out in my car. Oh, man, it was awful. James grabbed Ryan from the car and punched him over and over. As I watched, helpless and screaming, I felt tremendous guilt over Ryan getting beaten up. As their football coach broke it up, I could see Ryan was humiliated.

"When I went home that night, I debated which one to choose. Oddly enough, Ryan didn't have any anger toward me. He called to update me how he was and said James was a punk whose actions weren't my fault. I was completely relieved to hear him say that. When we hung up, I knew I needed to decide which one I'd be with and end the cheating. James made me feel so special and safe when we weren't fighting, which was about half the time we spent together. I'd walk into a room, and he'd say things like, 'there's my baby girl,' putting his arm around me. I felt incredibly special, loved, and like the luckiest girl in the room. Ryan wasn't so publicly charming, but he opened my car door, asked me questions, pursued a relationship with Jesus on his own, and genuinely cared about me. Plus he'd never once hurt or disrespected me. When I weighed the two guys out, I felt more drawn to James, which I hated. I knew, deep down, it wasn't right, but it was so hard to let go of the amazing feelings I had when we weren't fighting.

"The next day, James and I got into a screaming fight about Ryan and me. He said he'd take me back if I promised to never speak to Ryan again. Fearful of losing James completely, I impulsively agreed and promised. Later that night I called Ryan to tell him I still wanted to be with James and couldn't talk to him again. My throat tightened and I got nauseated as I heard Ryan's disappointment and confusion on the phone. He responded, 'Okay, Whit, if he makes you happy, then that's what I want, too.'

"When I look back, I'm not proud of those decisions but they taught me a lot. You're not alone in your struggle, Grace, and your struggle is not who you are," I said, grateful that my confession was over.

Grace grabbed a tissue off the table and blew her nose.

"Wow, you, *The* Whitney Roehl was a player and heartbreaker in school?" Grace said, kind of laughing with more lightness in her.

I hated to hear those words come out of her mouth and being associated with that, but I was glad she was feeling better. "I'm so glad you find that humorous. It wasn't for me at the time, but I know you already know that."

Grace was a smart girl, and I knew her current promiscuous struggle wasn't who she wanted to be. I also knew she was trying to find her worth in these boys. I knew because I was guilty of it back then too.

"Heartbreaker aside, can you please help me understand why you chose that stupid and probably ugly punk James over sweet Ryan? That seems like such an obvious choice," Grace asked.

I felt relief at her question. It was exactly what I was hoping she'd wonder.

"Well, it's easy for you to see that choice as obvious because you see me as worthy. I didn't see myself as worthy back then. As a matter of fact, I saw myself as unworthy and not lovable because I had a lot of evidence from the trauma with my dad. I craved to feel special and wanted so badly to feel safe from someone else. Whenever James put his arm around me publicly and announced his affection, I got a dopamine hit of 'I'm worthy' with evidence of it. Ryan didn't give me that publicly, even though it was more genuine and real. Plus, the fighting James and I did was a familiar dysfunction to me from witnessing my parents. I didn't believe I deserved better than what I'd experienced. The bottom line was that if I was seeing myself as unconditionally loved by God, being hidden in Christ, then I'd be able to clearly see the way James treated me wasn't respectful, and I wouldn't have tolerated it. Does that make sense?" I hoped Grace was putting the pieces together and seeing where she was falling into the same trap that I had.

Grace stared at the ground. She'd stopped crying, and I could see that she was thinking it all over in her mind. She sighed loudly. "Yeah, I see how I'm trying to feel safe with these guys and gain my worth from them. It's hard though because over the last few years of us meeting, I've made improvements, but for some reason I keep feeling a strong desire to have guys want me. I know what they really want is sex, so I give it to them. Not all the time but recently more than I'd like to admit. When I do, in that moment, I feel powerful, safe, and loved. After it all, well, that's when I feel like an idiot, disgusted with myself, and guilty because it's not really who I want to be. I must have daddy-issues or something because I want to wait for my future husband, my 'God's best' that you've talked about, but it feels impossible. That's why I'm such an idiot." Grace looked frustrated and discouraged.

I believed that Grace wanted to stop having sex with guys, and she genuinely wanted to wait for the guy she was going to marry. It was clear that she was still believing lies about herself and that her behavior wouldn't change if she kept thinking poorly and walking in that shame.

"Grace, you are not your mistakes. You are incredibly loved and valuable despite what you do or don't do. I know it's hard to believe, but God's love for you doesn't change based on your performance. He loves you based on His grace and goodness—it's who He is. It's our duty to believe that. What if you started to believe that you're not your past mistakes, that you're worth waiting for and capable of saving yourself from now on for your God's best?"

"That doesn't feel true though," Grace said. "I feel like I'd be lying to myself because of my recent actions. I keep making the same mistake over and over. That's why I'm a hot mess and don't deserve a good God-fearing man. It's hopeless—there's no point in trying."

I paused, not wanting to keep sharing if Grace wasn't ready to receive the lesson that was being presented. I prayed inwardly, "God, you know what Grace needs to hear, give me your insight, patience, and compassion so she can receive Your wisdom and grace."

I could tell Grace was pondering it all, desperately wanting to find a solution so she wouldn't keep desiring the exact thing she didn't want to do.

"So, if you chose stupid, ugly James because you didn't have any self-worth and couldn't see how badly he treated you, then how did you improve your self-worth and get to where you are now?" Grace asked. Her phone rang in her purse. She grabbed it, looked at the caller ID, rolled her eyes, and chucked it back in her purse.

"That's a great question, Grace, and I'd love to tell you I learned that lesson at a young age, like your age. And that there's a simple formula to take, but I learned the hard way, and there is no formula with God. The good news is that Jesus is always the answer. He is the Way and the Truth. Pursuing a relationship with Him transforms the way you see yourself. For years I overflowed with such a strong anger from my inner pain that I consistently turned to rebelling, like a prodigal daughter. However, eventually I hit enough dead ends and had faced enough hard consequences that over a decade later I learned the change I craved began with deepening my personal relationship with Jesus and not just attending church on Sundays to check a box. Hear me correctly though. I don't mean I got my act together *first* before going to Him because that's religion and not a relationship. I mean I started to ask Jesus to come into my shameful, uncomfortable messes to help me over and over again.

"In this process, one of my most impactful decisions was to increase my knowledge about Jesus and His heavenly Kingdom. I attended the Bethel School of Supernatural Ministry, an online three-year program that I pursued as a part-time student. This took my faith, breakthrough, and relationship with Jesus to an entirely new level. I grew hungrier for Jesus and began reading scripture regularly, praying for miracles, and encountering even more evidence of God's goodness. From there, the Holy Spirit changed my lenses and the way I saw myself. I started to feel a sense of belonging to His Kingdom as a *daughter*, which replaced my old orphan mindset of unworthiness. Even though I still make mistakes, the Holy Spirit graciously continues doing the inner work, so I've been able to stop striving on my own. From that point, I started to see myself more and more from His perspective: lovable, worthy, and significant. No one had told me what I'm telling you. So I had to figure it out the long and hard way, but that's also okay because it's allowed me to help others do the same." I paused to make sure she was still listening and not bored.

Grace nodded as though she had read my mind.

"Eventually the way I saw myself was transformed to not only worthy and loved but also as a co-laborer to Jesus with the assistance and supernatural power of the Holy Spirit constantly with me. In this process I noticed my desires and old behaviors changed. I no longer wanted to date the same kind of guys who disrespected me or didn't pursue Jesus on their own. Many of my other desires changed too, like drinking alcohol, the people I hung out with, and where I got my worth. That was a long process that doesn't have to take *you* as long though. Does that answer your question?" I asked as I got up to grab water for both of us.

When I came back into the room Grace was writing on a back of a random piece of paper that looked like she found from her purse. I sat back down, setting down two glasses of water.

"Yes, it resonates. I know I already have a personal relationship with Jesus, but you said something I never realized. I've been trying to fix myself, believing that I'm broken and that I need to do things perfectly to feel worthy for Jesus's love. You said that's religion, not a relationship. I've been trying to make these inner changes all on my own, feeling shameful when I mess up and feeling like God's mad at me every time. I believed I had to correct my behavior on my own, but you made a great point—Jesus is the One who does that inner work; I just keep inviting Him in and renewing my mind according to His words. I'm sure you've said that to me hundreds of times before, but for some reason it finally clicked. The shame I felt for not doing it right was preventing me from writing in my diary about how I was thinking or feeling because it was too painful. So I'm making a note that says, 'Stop trying to fix yourself, Grace. Go to Jesus because He wants a relationship with you now.'" She finished writing, looked up with a smile, and gave me a big hug.

I was grateful she was feeling better and that my past failures were giving her hope. I squeezed her tight in my arms, looked at her, and said, "I'm glad that resonated with you. You're made in God's image: an overcomer, courageous, good, worthy, and significant. Grace, it's important that you know that in your mind but also in your heart. I love your hunger to grow even when it's hard. You are so loved by God, without condition, and He wants to pour out all His blessings on you. It's up to you to keep your hope in Him—a confident, optimistic expectation that good is coming based on God's goodness and His promises."

Grace left feeling lighter, and I was incredibly relieved. I thanked God for giving me the courage to share vulnerably and for giving me the insight into what she needed to hear. Then an overwhelming sense of gratitude washed over me like a wave. It felt as though God was saying, "I'm proud of you" and affirming the younger version of me who made the mistakes, saying, "I knew your path all along and my love never changed. I worked every traumatic experience and evil thing out for your good because you trust me, Whit. Today, you are witnessing the fruit of putting your trust in me, even when you couldn't see it working." This deep inner knowing that God reassigned my darkest moments with purpose and love felt incredibly freeing.

I prayed, "Thank You, Jesus, for Your death and resurrection that accomplished everything for me that I could never do for myself. What You did was enough. It is everything. Thank You for giving me strength today to accomplish your purpose. You pursued me in my darkest moments, and I know You will do the same for Grace. And I declare when I feel weak, I am strong. I pray this in Jesus's name. Amen."

*   *   *

You may have shame from your past that haunts you in the quiet moments and tempts you to question your worth. I carried shame for way too long. Listen, nothing—absolutely nothing—makes you unworthy or justifies you carrying around something so toxic as shame that Jesus already paid the debt for. He already accomplished what you and I couldn't so that we could live free from that self-hatred and condemnation.

I've worked with a handful of women who've had traumatic experiences, reacting to their current life events from the shame, guilt, and fear they still carry. If you have a hard time forgiving yourself for current mistakes, letting go of your past, consistently look for outside validation to feel worthy, or feeling shame regularly, then inviting Holy Spirit to change the way you see yourself would be a great first step. I'll share more on how to do that in the "consider this" section.

Being a high achiever with a type A personality, I fell into the trap that when I achieve the body, money, marriage, and life that I want, then I will finally like who I am and experience less shame and unworthiness. It never works that way. I've witnessed others fall into this trap over and over. You have to deal with the shame head on by repenting for the shame you're holding on to, praying something like this: "Heavenly Father, I ask for You forgiveness for allowing shame to have a voice, my lack of belief that my sins are forgiven, and forgive me for the negative view I've had of myself. In Jesus Name. Amen." Then spend time declaring God's Truth over yourself, agreeing with who He says you are.

If we don't address the shame, then we self-sabotage, numbing it with alcohol, food, or busyness, and stuck in a vicious cycle that literally ruins relationships, even marriages.

That self-condemning voice gets so loud and relentlessly questions your purpose, worth, and identity, no matter your accomplishments.

CONSIDER THIS

My old self has been crucified with Christ. It is no longer I who live, but Christ lives in me. So I live in this earthly body by trusting in the Son of God, who loved me and gave himself for me. (Gal. 2:20)

The way you choose to see yourself is one of the most impactful decisions you'll ever make—your identity. How you think about yourself matters. If you see yourself as "not good enough," then you'll constantly show up feeling "not good enough."

You are made in God's image—incredibly unique, priceless, and completely "good enough." You won't see yourself from His perspective until you choose it on purpose, and it moves down to your heart until you feel it in your bones.

Galatians 3:27 says, "And all who have been united with Christ in baptism have put on Christ, like putting on new clothes."

Maybe you need to put on these new clothes—as a son or daughter of God the Creator of the heavens and Earth. To do so, you'll want to take off your old clothes, whatever fear or shame-based ways you've viewed yourself need to be taken off before you can put the new clothes on.

Take some time right now to ask the Holy Spirit, "In what ways am I seeing myself disconnected from Jesus's love?" Write down whatever comes to your mind—don't overthink it. Then ask the Holy Spirit, "How do you want me to see myself?"

Then, say these truths the Holy Spirit shared with you out loud, declaring them over yourself, and inviting the Holy

Spirit to come in revolutionary power, and show you how wide, high, and deep the Father's love is for you. It's your job to resist the enemy and receive these truths. Once you get a taste of this freedom, you'll become hungrier for Him! The nature of God's goodness is beyond our imagination. Taste it and see for yourself.

CHAPTER THREE

Facing Your Shame

I PARKED MY CAR IN the hospital parking lot near the emergency room entrance with my heart pounding. I sprinted into the building, and when I found Grace's mom, Stacy, we locked eyes. She looked distressed and unsure of what to do. I ran over to her and hugged her.

Immediately she collapsed in my arms, crying hysterically. "Whit, I can't lose my baby," she said.

I could barely put together her words but felt her desperation.

For the next hour, Stacy and I sat in the waiting room as we prayed for Grace. I didn't have any details on how Grace was doing yet because I didn't want to ask, and we were waiting on the doctors to update us. It was two o'clock in the morning when Stacy had called to tell me Grace was being rushed to the ER and needed me to meet her there. I didn't get more information but just assumed Grace was in a car accident or something. She was so fit and active that I was certain it wasn't a health issue.

Stacy was calmer but an underlying anxiety was still very present, so I went to grab us both a water bottle and returned to wait with her.

"I don't know what I did wrong," she said, staring at the floor.

Not sure if asking questions was a good idea, I chose to go for it. "Do you know what happened?"

She didn't say anything, and I questioned if she'd heard me.

Then she responded, "I heard a loud thud downstairs in Grace's room. It sounded like someone hit their head on the concrete floor. It was so loud it woke me up. So I got up to make sure Grace was home and everything was okay." She paused, tears running down her face.

I put my hand on her arm hoping to help her feel supported.

"She was there on the floor, in front of her bed. I ran over to see what was wrong and saw an empty pill bottle next to her. I shook her body, yelling her name. Nothing. No response. So I ran upstairs to get my phone, called 911, and ran back downstairs to be with her. When I came back down luckily, I got there just in enough time to see her vomiting on her back. So I rolled her on her side so she wouldn't choke, but she was still completely incoherent. Whitney, I can't tell you the amount of regret and guilt that piled on while I waited for the ambulance to get there. All this time I've spent drinking to numb the anger and hurt I've held toward her dad. Grace would yell at me that I'm never there for her and that I'm too preoccupied with drinking. I couldn't ever see it. But in that moment, while I watched her looking lifeless on the cold concrete floor, it hit me like a ton of bricks. She was right. She was right. I'm a horrible mother. I'm an idiot for letting my own past pain steal one of my greatest blessings." Stacy's crying turned back into a hysterical cry with a weight of hopelessness.

I was trying to do my best to stay present for Stacy, but inside I felt anger toward her on behalf of Grace. Over the years, Grace had shared stories of the hurt and rejection she'd felt from her mom. In this moment, unsure of Grace's life, the anger I'd deflected toward her mom washed over me. I breathed in deeply. "God, I need your strength, wisdom, and hope to refresh me," I prayed inwardly. Rubbing Stacy's back, I didn't say anything to comfort her. All I could do was be present and pray.

What seemed like hours later, a doctor walked into the waiting room toward us. "Mrs. Lee, I have an update about your daughter," the doctor said, looking hopeful but stone-faced. He was a tall man with dark hair and olive skin, very handsome, but looked like he was strictly business and with little bedside manner.

I put my hand on Stacy's back to comfort her and myself.

"Grace is going to live, but she's still incoherent. This is a very serious matter. If she would have gotten to us just a few seconds later, there wouldn't have been anything we could have done. This was a miracle today. You can go into her room now, but we'll need to transfer her to a different room when we can. She'll be admitted to the hospital for several days so we can monitor her recovery. We will want to talk about admitting her to a mental health treatment center after she is discharged from here. We take this matter very seriously," the doctor informed us with a very stern, almost cold, voice.

While the doctor continued talking, all I could think about was a world without Grace. She was too young, she had an entire life to live, and God's purpose was so big on her life. I didn't understand how Grace couldn't see her awesomeness, how many people she impacted, the light she carried, and how many people loved her.

I backtracked to our most recent visits. How had I not seen these suicidal symptoms? The last time I saw her was only three or four weeks earlier. She'd stopped by on her way home to share the message from her Wednesday night youth group because it'd gotten her hopeful about a family challenge she was going through.

Grace was always putting a lot of expectations and unnecessary pressure on herself. When she made mistakes, her self-condemnation and shame were two of the hardest struggles I helped her work through, but she had seemed to be getting a handle on it—or so I thought.

Questions flooded my mind. Was there a recent event that caused this? Was she not telling me the full truth about her life? Were there things she didn't want me to know?

"God, please heal Grace. Heal her mind, body, and spirit from the harm of this suicide attempt. Please allow her to experience Your unconditional love for her. I love her so much, God, and I know You do too," I prayed.

"Whit, Whit." Stacy said. "The doctor said we can go in. I'm going to grab my purse and jacket, and we'll head in there."

The doctor led us to Grace's room. I was bracing myself, expecting the worst but hoping for the best. The moment I saw the IVs attached to her arms and her sleeping, tears streamed down my face, and my chest and throat tightened. My love for Grace felt so big it hurt. I was no longer there to support Stacy—I was now there for me. Grace and I had grown so close over the last four years, and she was becoming the daughter I'd never had.

I walked to the side of her bed and gently ran my fingers through her hair. She loved when I did anything with her hair. Seeing her in that hospital room had such a cold effect in my heart. I felt heavy inside, like a huge burden was weighing me down.

"You didn't do enough, Whit," I thought. "You've been here before, in her place, and still didn't prevent this from happening. Good role models don't mentor people who attempt to end their life." My mind chatter got louder and louder as the guilt stirred up in my stomach.

I flashed back to the hospital room where I'd been when I was her age, in the exact same situation she was in, but I didn't have a mentor who visited me. Only one guy friend from high school knew about my suicide attempt.

"If you were more honest with Grace about your past then this wouldn't have happened," I thought, and I was so overwhelmed that I excused myself and walked into the hallway.

I took a deep breath and redirected my focus. "I'm not Grace's savior—only Jesus is. I'm not in Grace's life to fix her because she doesn't need fixing. My job is not and never was to prevent Grace from going on her own journey. God has worked all things to work for my good because I trust Him, and He will do the same for Grace. My job is only to love her in every season. It's Christ in me who shines, not me. The Holy Spirit in me is working powerfully to help those around me according to His power not mine," I fiercely reminded myself.

I spent the next four hours at the hospital waiting for Grace to wake up before I headed home to get some sleep. The doctors had assured Stacy and me multiple times that Grace was recovering and that it was just going to take some time since her body was still in shock.

When I got home, I was emotionally and physically exhausted. I knew I wouldn't be able to sleep—still feeling my adrenaline—but showering and spending some time in prayer with worship music would help. After showering, I poured a cup of hot peppermint tea, put my headphones in to worship music, and sat there like a zombie.

Even though I knew Grace would live, there was a lingering feeling as though she'd died. Logically, I knew it wasn't reality, but emotionally I couldn't shake the shock of not knowing whether she'd live or not. I wanted to sob. I gave myself permission to let it all out. I wept and wept and wept. It was as though the Lord was healing the young teenage girl inside of me who was emotionally hurting like I knew Grace was. The heaviness of the shame and unworthiness was real, a true oppression spiritually and emotionally.

I could feel that version of me who was still hurting from the physical and emotional abuse I'd suffered as a kid. The girl who felt all the pressure of needing to be perfect to stay safe. The girl who always expected the other shoe to drop, expected the worse to happen because nine out of ten times it did. The girl who ran for safety over and over, who spent her life building self-protective walls to survive. Even though Grace hadn't experienced the childhood trauma I had, I knew the emotional neglect from her parents was harming her, and the rebellious choices she made trapped her in a prison of shame.

The worship music shifted my heart and thoughts, redirecting them to Jesus. I sang out loud, knowing the outward worship would change my inner experience. "All hail King Jesus. All hail the Savior of the world. All hail King Jesus." As I sang those words over and over, my tears turned from hopelessness to hope filled. I stayed in worship on my knees, my hands lifted, singing at the top of my lungs as though I was declaring these words over my own mind and soul as well as Grace's. Finally, my lack of sleep hit me, and I dozed off peacefully after worshipping the Lord of my life, Jesus.

*   *   *

Later that week, I visited Grace, and she was expected to be discharged from the hospital. She'd made incredibly progress in her recovery, and we'd had some in-depth conversations. She and her mom had had some reconciliation and healing conversations too. I could already see the miracles taking place, and I was incredibly grateful for so many prayers being answered.

"Thanks for being there for my mom through all this," Grace said, almost fully back to her normal, spunky self.

"Of course. It was good for us both. Now please promise me this whole suicide attempt won't happen again, right?" I asked boldly. It was on my mind, just to clarify, that we both were on the same page that this scare was hard on all of us. I wanted to reiterate to Grace how devastating it was for us to face the reality of her no longer living if the doctors hadn't been successful.

Grace looked me in the eyes with tears in her eyes and said, "I'm sorry. This was scary for me too. I didn't realize how permanent this one decision could have been. Do you think God's mad at me?" She asked, pulling the bedsheet closer to her neck as though she was trying to become invisible.

"Absolutely not, Grace. God isn't mad. Remember, your relationship with Jesus isn't any different from your relationship with me—except He's all powerful. He wants you to be honest and real like you are with me. There's nothing you can hide from Him, but He wants you to share the good and the ugly with Him. When you are hurting, worried, or fearful, talk to Him. Our Heavenly Dad is always moved by compassion and His perfection to respond. God works all things out for our good because we trust Him. Someday this will be a powerful testimony you'll be able to share with someone else who is experiencing what you went through. Then you can share the goodness of our Father and Jesus's radical love, right?"

I knew her eyes had been opened in a new way, and that gave me a lot of peace. I gave her a big hug and was so grateful I'd been able to be with her through this dark moment. When I didn't have anyone, I felt God giving me an opportunity to love someone else through their pain.

"Thanks God, for the wisdom and blessings You've given me through my own healing journey. Even when it's painful, the fruit of going through the dark moments are always worth it with You by my side. You're the reason I'm alive, Jesus. I trust You today and forever," I said inwardly to God.

*   *   *

As I drove home that day from visiting Grace at the hospital, the memories flashed through my mind.

During my four years of high school, on the outside looking in, I had it all. I was well liked. I played varsity sports, served on student council, and participated in FCA (Fellowship of Christian Athletes). Inside though, I felt like I was dying slowly, like I couldn't breathe in enough oxygen. There was a constant pressure on my chest, like I was seconds away from having a full-blown panic attack. My senior year, I experienced a depression I was unaware of.

"I can't do this anymore. The pain is too intense. It'd be better to just go to sleep…forever. It's not worth fighting anymore," I thought. The sneaky part about this moment was that I didn't see the thoughts as suicidal. I saw them as just facts—it'd be better for myself and everyone else if I was gone.

The deception and sneakiness of the accuser was real. These spiritual attacks came disguised in sheep's clothing, looking and seeming innocent. At the time, I didn't even feel depressed, just really emotionally exhausted with an internal pain I couldn't seem to relieve. I was ashamed of how weak I felt and who I'd become. It seemed like my path back to the young girl I liked that I once knew in middle school was so far away that it wasn't even worth considering. I didn't know who this new girl was, I didn't like myself, and my friends who were all partying and having sex with others didn't seem to care or seem bothered by their choices. I, on the other hand, felt a tremendous amount of guilt and condemnation, but for some reason, I couldn't stop falling back into the same patterns.

I learned that thoughts like "people would be better off without me" or "I just want to go to sleep forever" don't come from God. They are strategies from the enemy whose only interest is to steal from, kill, and destroy people. If I would have known that back then, I wouldn't have fallen into the trap. Instead, I would have fought back in prayer or asked for help.

It's a hard topic to be open about: attempting to end your life to the point of being in the hospital. But I feel God wanting me to bring this darkness to the light, so He can begin to heal wounds in others that need His love and power.

I can still remember the doctor's condemning voice, "If you hadn't gotten here when you did, you wouldn't be alive right now. Do you know how serious this was?"

I felt a new cloak of shame cover my body. I wanted to crawl out of my own skin and never see anyone again. The hardest people to face were my parents. I could see the disappointment written all over their faces. They had no clue I was feeling so much inner pain and were confused why ending my life was even a solution at all.

When I look back to this dark and shame-filled time of my life, I want to walk into that hospital room, tell everyone to leave, and give my younger self a long bear hug. I was in a lot of emotional pain but didn't even know it. On top of that, I put tons of pressure on myself to "have it all together." Being popular wasn't easy.

I would tell my younger self, "It's good to ask for help. That doesn't mean you're weak or broken—releasing these things is a healthy part of life. So be kind to yourself. You'll get through this, Whit."

Of course, it's easier to give your younger self advice and support because you've come out of the tunnel on the other side, knowing "it all works." But I've learned it's still an important thing to remember to love the younger version of myself who tried to take her life. Otherwise, the condemnation would continue to follow me everywhere.

As it was, shame *did* follow me. At the time, I hated my past, which was a part of me. Shame followed me for the next ten years, and I didn't even know it. I'd become so familiar with it that it was like being covered in stinky mud but being so used to the smell I forgot it was mud. You never wash it off because it feels just a part of who you are. I spent my twenties running from this awful feeling without realizing it. I'd move to new places, date new guys, change anything and everything I could, thinking "a new start" was all I needed.

Every time I began the healing process, I'd get distracted by all those new things and never slow down to look inward to do the deeper work. These distractions were not bad in themselves, but they kept me busy, preoccupied, and continuing the same old patterns that kept me numbing instead of healing.

Since my attempted suicide, I've known five people who ended their life and a handful of people who've personally reached out sharing they "don't feel living life is worth it anymore and want to end it." I'm honored by people's honesty and trust, but I hate the enemy's evil strategy behind these thoughts. Those suicidal thoughts are straight from the pit of hell.

*   *   *

When I look back on these stories of pain, suffering, and heartache, I no longer see them drenched in judgment and condemnation. I see these stories with compassion and a genuine love for myself. Getting to this place of inner freedom has been a long journey of healing with Jesus and of learning self-forgiveness.

As I write these stories out, reliving them from a distance, I can see more clearly than ever before that Jesus was re-writing my story. He loves *all* of me. He loved me then, in my sin and pain, and He loves me now, in my freedom and healing. I don't believe He caused me to suffer or wanted me to make harmful decisions, but He knew I would, and it didn't change His love for me.

That's the power of His radical and reckless love, a love you and I could never earn even if we could live a perfect life. When I'd run from my pain, I wasn't aware of His love. I believed for so long that I had to fix myself first and then I'd be "good enough" to be a follower of Jesus. This deception is a strategy from Satan. He doesn't want us to believe that Jesus gives us His grace freely and loves us unconditionally because then Satan's attacks of shame, guilt, and condemnation would stop working.

I pray that your eyes are opened to the Father's love for you. It doesn't matter where you are in life, what you've done, or what sin or struggle you might be battling. His love is not— and never was—based on your performance. He is waiting for you, with arms wide open. My friend, I pray for your healing and that if you're a runner like I am, you stay put long enough for Him to do the deeper work in your heart. He is worthy of trusting. He is faithful and good. I pray you have courage to face your fears and endure the freedom process He wants to take you on. You are so loved, my dear friend—so loved! Amen.

CONSIDER THIS

I tell you, you can pray for anything, and if you believe that you've received it, it will be yours. But when you are praying, first forgive anyone you are holding a grudge against, so that your Father in Heaven will forgive your sins, too. (Mark 11:24–25)

One of the biggest reasons I stayed stuck for so many years was that I was completely unaware and ignorant to the power of forgiveness. I never knew that holding on to past offenses was even called unforgiveness. I didn't know the spiritual power it had and how it manifests in the physical realm. I was clueless that holding on to offenses allowed the demonic realm to access your mind, body, and spirit. After learning the power and consequences to forgiveness, I went through an extensive process with a mentor to forgive people from my childhood all the way up to my current life. It took a few weeks because as I forgave these people I wept, grieving the pain, but I also felt chains of heaviness being broken. I'd lived with so much anger and inner rage that I believed it was just part of my personality. It wasn't. I'm no longer an angry person and barely ever get mad. That's so different from one point of my life punching holes in a door. I also had believed the lie that staying offended with the people who hurt me kept me safe. It didn't. Instead, it kept me bitter and repelling God's love.

Now, I know that forgiveness is one of the most foundational parts of the healing process and the ability to walking in freedom. It's where I start, checking to see if there's anyone I need to forgive (whether it's a big or small offense). I'll share the forgiveness prayer my spiritual mom gave me that I've shared with several people. She described it perfectly: "the forgiveness prayer is like a sword. It's heavy to pick up, but when you pick it up to use it you can cut through anything that's not for you. It's mighty and powerful."

Remember, your pain has a purpose. But transformation will require you to face your pain, release it, and exchange it for something good. Your biggest advocate in this process is Jesus. Invite Him to exchange your pain for His peace. You can take your first step, today.

Ask the Holy Spirit, "Is there anyone I need to forgive?" Write down anyone who comes to mind. Then ask the Holy Spirit, "Please give me the courage and strength to forgive the people who came to mind through the prayer below." You can expect that Jesus will be right next to you as you let go of these offenses you've been holding. It's normal if you need to say this prayer multiple times before you feel the freedom. It's also common for relationships to be restored, health to be restored, and doors of opportunity to open because forgiveness is a mighty tool in the Kingdom.

Heavenly Father, I confess I am offended with [Name]. I felt [tell God the painful emotional and physical feelings provoked], and I also judged that [tell God what you assumed about the person]. Nevertheless, in spite of these feelings and judgments and with hope and faith in the great love You cherish for me and what You alone can do in my soul, I choose to forgive [Name] unconditionally. I loose him/her and let him/her go. He/She owes me no debt.

Holy Spirit, please show me any other offense I need to forgive him/her for [pause, and if any other offense comes up, start this prayer from the beginning until no other offense comes to mind]. In the name of Jesus I drop all my charges against [Name] and lay aside all of my judgments provoked by these offenses. I release [Name] from all responsibility to me regarding these offenses. I renounce every negative word spoken by [Name] to me and me to him/her. Those words are null and void. In the name of Jesus I break their power over both of us. I also renounce every other negative effect this offense has had on my spirit, soul, or body. Holy Spirit, please come now and heal my thoughts and emotions. Thank You, Lord, for completing what I have begun in faith. Amen.[1]

Awesome work! Keep this prayer somewhere close by so you can refer to it as often as you need. I still use it on a weekly basis because I don't ever want to have even a small offense harbor anger in my mind, body, or spirit that leads to reoccurring negative emotions and heavy burdens.

The final step is to build a stronghold of compassion for the person you have forgiven.

---

[1] Paraclaysis Ministries

CHAPTER FOUR

Faith First

I T WAS A JOY OF mine to visit the city of Chicago, a city I had lived in for several years for seasons filled with both growing pains and good times. This Christmas I decided to visit to enjoy the light festival on The Magnificent Mile, the people, and the wonderful restaurants. Plus it felt a bit nostalgic from my twenties. I decided to spend a few days over the weekend to shop, dine, walk around, and work on my second book.

During my flight out there, while being engrossed in reading and taking notes, I got a surprising text from Grace: "Hey, Whit! Exciting news, I'm in New York now visiting a friend, and he wants to fly us out to Chicago tomorrow. He said he HAS to meet you before Christmas. I'll text you when we arrive. Let's grab dinner. Love you." I had casually mentioned in a previous text that I was making this quick trip but didn't hear anything back, so I had figured she was busy, and I hoped to see her around Christmas.

Still, I felt uneasy. Because Grace was now a sophomore in college, I didn't see her as regularly as when she was in high school. We'd meet for coffee every time she was in town, but over the last two years, we only saw each other face-to-face a handful of times. Outside of that, we texted regularly, but somehow, I still felt like I was missing what was really going on in her life.

The most recent time we chatted, she was venting about her frustration toward her mom not supporting her siblings during their sports and events. She felt guilty for not being able to visit them more frequently, like she'd neglected them. I loved hearing Grace's heart for her siblings but did my best to remind her that God would be their Protector and Comforter like He was for her. I reminded her to trust Him. Because we hadn't talked since that conversation, I felt a bit unsettled about this new "friend" that sounded serious.

I prayed quietly, "God, thank You for aligning Grace's and my schedules so we can see each other. Thank You that You're working in her life, even when I don't see it because You love her. Give me Your wisdom and discernment when I see her and meet this new guy friend of hers." Then, I texted her, "What a fun surprise, Gracie! Dinner tomorrow sounds great. Love you, too."

When I walked into my hotel room at the Trump International Hotel, I was overwhelmed with joy to see the floor-to-ceiling windows and beautiful nighttime skyline from the fifty-sixth floor. The views in Chicago were breathtaking and some of my favorite. It felt great to be back visiting.

Looking at the view, I had a wave of feeling a great amount of success. I'd dreamed of being able to stay at hotels like this when traveling, but I never believed it'd be possible this young. The previous years when visiting Chicago, I'd save my money to spend toward shopping, but that year my business had done exceptionally well.

One thing I consistently do when I travel is pack a candle and lighter to have in the room to relax. Smell is everything to me—it either creates peace or anxiety. I've learned to never assume nice hotels smell delightful. I lit the candle, turned on my "God's Presence" playlist, made a bubble bath, and poured some S. Pellegrino sparkling water in one of their fancy glasses.

Fully indulging in my experience, I asked out loud, "God, why am I so blessed?"

My conversations with God are usually inward or in my journal, unless I'm alone, and then I prefer to talk to Him out loud. I feel closer to Him that way, reminding myself He is always with me.

I heard Him say, "You're blessed because you built your life on the solid foundation of my Son."

It felt so peaceful to receive that, knowing that wasn't always the case and had taken me years of seeking Him and desiring His Presence more than my own desires. It was truly another evidence of Jesus's inner work, and I was incredibly grateful for it. I knew in my spirit that I'd always savor this moment. It meant so much to me to be in Chicago, feeling the strongest I'd ever felt in my relationship with God, free of strongholds and more steadfast in my faith. The success and financial wealth were just icing on the cake.

That night I went to sleep with anticipation and excitement for seeing Grace, but also with a deep inner peace like a warm blanket covering me, relaxing me from the inside out. "I'll get her a present while shopping tomorrow," I thought, then drifted off to sleep.

My morning routine, even when I travel, stays consistent. I do some form of quick exercise, then grab water and a cup of coffee to sit down with my journal, Bible, and declarations. All of it usually takes me about two hours in total. If I don't do it in the morning I feel out of sorts and usually end up feeling irritable and distracted, so I've learned how to keep it simple especially when traveling.

After I completed my routine, I didn't have any set plans, other than shopping for Christmas gifts and, of course, anything I saw for myself. I had an idea of a cute gift Grace would like, so I went to the little boutique and grabbed it. When I visited Chicago this time of year, I let myself spend a decent amount of money and refused to judge myself. Gift giving is one of my love languages; plus splurging in Chicago this time of year was how I enjoyed celebrating another amazing year.

After a few hours of shopping on The Magnificent Mile and only having coffee for breakfast, I was starving, so I stopped by a little café in the Gold Coast area for a bite to eat. My phone buzzed with a text from Grace: "Hey, Whit, we landed! We'll check into our hotel, shower and be ready for dinner at 5:30. I know you prefer to eat an earlier dinner. I'll make us three reservations at Chicago Cut Steakhouse. See you then."

I hearted the message and put my phone back in my purse.

My mind wondered about this guy friend. Grace was being brief, like she didn't want me to ask too many questions. Usually our texting was a bit more back and forth, and this time it just felt a bit off. "I'm probably overthinking and blaming it on this guy," I thought. For the rest of the day, I tried to stay present and not indulge in worry. I reminded myself that no matter what, God was actively working in Grace's life.

At five o'clock, after getting dressed in a high-waisted black jumpsuit and leather jacket with stilettos, I walked downstairs to get in a cab. I wanted to get to the restaurant early to settle in, relax, and not rush into dinner.

When I walked into the bar area, to my complete surprise I saw Grace had cut her long red hair short to her jawline. From behind her, I could see she was wearing a golden skin-tight sequined minidress. She looked gorgeous from my angle but ten years older the way she was styled. Excited to see her,

I walked up and gave her a big squeeze from behind, completely forgetting about the guy she was with.

"Aww, Whit. It's so good to see you!" She spun around in her high-top chair, got down, and gave me an even bigger hug. She was wearing bright red lipstick and tall stilettos. I don't know that I'd ever seen Grace dressed this way before. She was always stylish but in more of an athletic and surfer look, even for fancy steak houses.

"Wow, Grace! You look..." I paused, looking her up and down. "You look...so mature and gorgeous."

She smiled. "You have to meet my boyfriend, Vincent," Grace said, turning around to introduce me to the older guy beside her.

"It's so nice to meet you, Whitney. After hearing from Gracie how much you've changed her life, I told her we'll do whatever we have to so I can meet you before flying Gracie to meet my family over Christmas," he said, firmly shaking my hand.

I was immediately impressed with how charming and likable Vincent was, but I felt that same uneasiness as on the plane. Two things jumped out as being odd. She'd said, "boyfriend," but she'd never mentioned that she was even seeing a guy. I thought it was strange she would hide such a big and exciting change. Second, why was he calling her *Gracie*? I was the only one who, on occasion, called her *Gracie*.

"It's nice to meet you too, Vincent. I look forward to hearing all the details of how you two met." As I was finishing my sentence, Vincent waved the bartender down.

"Johnny, we need to settle up. Put it on my card and bring it to our table. Thanks, man," he ordered, as though he and Johnny had been long time friends, but from Johnny's expression I could tell that was not the case. "Okay, ladies, let's head to our table. Whitney, I made sure they gave us the best window seat since I understand you love the Chicago views," he said, ushering us ahead.

Already, I was very impressed with Vincent's leadership, but at the same time I had so many questions racing through my mind. I wanted discernment without judging too soon. I prayed inwardly, "God, I need You to guide me during this dinner."

"Vincent, I'm impressed with the way you run the show. How old are you?" I asked boldly, unafraid to cut to the chase.

Grace laughed with a bit of embarrassment, knowing I'm not one to beat around the bush.

"Thank you, Whitney. I've had a lot of experience with people, you could say. I'm thirty-six, and your questions don't bother me one bit. Gracie warned me before dinner that you like to ask a lot of in-depth questions," he said, smiling.

As we sat down, I sensed that Grace and Vincent were more serious than they were letting on. While my questions were racing to come out, I had to pause and enjoy the beautiful view. Vincent was right—we had the best view in the entire restaurant. We were right on the river, with a view of the city and all the dazzling Christmas lights. I reminded myself to relax and let God guide me, so I didn't turn our dinner into proving or disproving whether Vincent was God's best for Grace.

The waiter came by and took our drink order. Vincent was kind to order me the best sparkling water in a wine glass and a bottle of Caymus Cabernet (from Napa Valley) for Grace and himself. I could tell Grace was already tipsy from the drinks they must have had at the bar earlier. She'd shared with me years before how she tends to use alcohol to feel more comfortable in social settings, and she was concerned about the alcoholism on both sides of her family.

"Vincent, how did you and Grace meet?" I asked, trying my hardest not to make any assumptions but stay curious and lighthearted.

"That's a great question and one of my favorites. I was visiting her college town with some business partners. We were craving some sushi, so we decided to walk to the closest restaurant to our hotel. That's where I saw Grace eating by herself and reading a book. I was impressed and intrigued that such a beautiful young lady was choosing to eat alone. Right away, I wanted to know more about her. After I ordered my food, I walked over to her table and sat across from her." Vincent paused, swirled the wine in his glass, took a sip, then smiled.

"Of course, Gracie didn't make it easy for me to make conversation with her. She has some walls you have to break through, but after thirty minutes or so she couldn't resist my charm and good looks." He looked over to Grace sitting next to him and kissed her on the cheek.

"He was persistent and made me laugh. I mean, he *is* handsome, but Whit knows I need way more than good looks to give a guy my time," Grace responded, looking at Vincent then back at me. I noticed neither of them spoke about how God had led or was leading their relationship. It concerned me that the relationship Grace was in didn't have Jesus at the center of it once again, that she was going down a familiar path of getting her worth and significance from Vincent.

I continued to listen to them share how their dates turned into more dates and how they got to being exclusive. I was taking it all in, bit by bit, wanting just to be supportive to Grace and get to know Vincent from an unbiased place.

"I'm going to the ladies' room," Grace said, getting up from the table.

Vincent watched Grace get up and walk away, not taking his eyes off her for a second. It was almost like he wanted to be sure no other guy looked or talked to her. It was a very protective but borderline controlling gaze.

"Do you love her?" I asked boldly, knowing his answer would be a definite *yes*. I was more curious about the way he would respond, his words, and tone.

Vincent paused, turned to look at me, then paused again. He leaned in over the table, like he was going to whisper a secret to me. "I could have any woman I wanted," he fiercely stated, "but *I want* Grace. She's bright, beautiful, and full of life. Plus, she lets me be the leader in our relationship. You know, be the man. I want a confident woman who will still submit to me. Grace makes me feel alive when I'm with her. That's what I deserve. So, yes. Yes, I love her, and I will marry her." He sat back in his chair, smiled as though he had no interest in really winning me over or what I thought, then swallowed the last of his wine.

Grace was already making her way back to the table before I could say anything back to Vincent. I didn't need him to win me over or prove anything to me. I cared about His relationship with Jesus and if he was an honorable man—that's it. Both of those values seemed up for debate.

"That was fast," I said with a tinge of disappointment that Vincent and I hadn't had more time to talk. I genuinely was curious about this man who claimed to love such a special woman. He was smart for choosing her.

As Grace sat down, Vincent turned to kiss her on the cheek, while scanning the room to see if other guys saw him claiming her. Instantly, I felt uneasy with memories that followed. It was his seemingly controlling affection toward Grace that I recognized from my past. I hadn't been able to put my finger on it until this moment.

Memories flooded me with the feeling of working and living in downtown Chicago, full of energy with all the beautiful tall buildings. I'd gotten a job as a cocktail server in one of the hottest new bars in River North off LaSalle street. I'd never served drinks before, barely twenty-two years old, and loving the night-life lifestyle. I made good money, lots of cash and after work I frequented the night clubs with coworkers until three in the morning. It was a blast!

Within six months of moving to Chicago, at our company holiday party, I was introduced to a handsome Venezuelan guy— Anthony. He instantly grabbed my attention. He moved to Chicago a few years ago to help his brother open a bar. It was the first time I'd met someone who was so different in culture, appearance, and even language. His English was pretty broken with a thick accent. I was instantly intrigued, and for some odd reason, I felt challenged to make him fall in love with me, probably because I doubted a guy like him would be interested in me.

"Hi, I'm Whitney, one of the cocktail servers at the new bar," I said smiling ear to ear and putting my hand out to shake his.

"I know who you are," Anthony said confidently without smiling and shook my hand.

"How do you know my name?" I asked.

He was wearing a black sports jacket, white undershirt, with what looked like very expensive jeans. I was impressed with his style, and he was surprisingly very suave.

"My brother knows the owner of the bar you work at, and I asked him about you," he said loudly over the music. Even with the loud setting and my difficulty understanding his accent, we talked for the rest of the night. That was the beginning of a life-changing relationship. We dated for a year before he proposed to me during our week-long vacation to New York City.

Our relationship was a hot passionate roller coaster. We both loved to eat at fancy places, dance at night clubs, and worked in the bar industry till the late hours. He was a manager, soon to be part owner, and I was a cocktail server promoted to bartender. We worked hard and played hard. We weren't rich by any means, but the cash that came in every week was addicting. Our work paid for the lifestyle we craved. I loved dressing up fancy and slinging drinks in one of the most popular downtown bars. He loved that we worked close enough together—he could keep an eye on me. Plus, we both did one thing really well together—party.

Our cultural differences and language barrier made communicating extremely challenging. He often got jealous, and those outbursts would end with fits of anger and a hole punched in the wall or door. I was used to that kind of relationship though since I grew up watching my dad do things like that. For the most part, it didn't bother me.

Later, when Anthony and I had been engaged for a year, and it was three months before our wedding, we were living together in a beautiful high-rise apartment on the twenty-first floor, right on Lake Michigan. It wasn't how I'd imagined my relationship would be before getting married. I remember telling Mr. and Mrs. Johnson one day at their dinner table that I wanted my future husband to love Jesus on his own, just like they both loved Jesus individually. Anthony wasn't a believer though. He grew up Catholic in Venezuela, going to church because his parents enforced it, but he didn't desire to have a personal relationship with Jesus. It was a recurring argument we'd had throughout our engagement.

Since I liked the financial security of living with him, I let that take priority over other values, like waiting until after marriage to live with a guy. The fear of being poor was real for me, even though I made a decent living bartending. I would rather have the security of a wealthy lifestyle than pursue Jesus when I knew He'd forgive me.

We were on our way to a nice dinner just a few blocks from our apartment. I was wearing a dress and stilettos, so we took a cab instead of his motorcycle, which I loved to ride.

"Babe, I don't want other guys looking at you with that dress on," Anthony said in his Venezuelan accent, putting his hand on my thigh.

I suspected he'd make a comment about my dress, but I assumed it wouldn't be until after he'd had a glass or two of wine at dinner. Feeling irritated that his controlling comments started early, I looked at him. "You're about to marry a beautiful woman, Anthony, so you'd better get used to it," I said in a playful but agitated tone, risking an angered response.

"Ugh, there you go again. I'm marrying a beautiful woman, but I refuse to be nice when stupid men look at you with hungry eyes. They offends me," he said sternly. Born and raised in Venezuela until he was eighteen, Anthony still spoke broken English when was angry.

I didn't want to get into an argument this early in the night, so I chose to not say anything, which felt harder at times when my frustration grew this high. "Well then don't be offended," I said and kissed him on the cheek.

Getting out of the cab, Anthony turned to help me out, then pulled my hip closely to his and kept his arm around me. Instantly, he seemed arrogant and rude. As the bouncer to the restaurant opened the door, I smiled, looking at Anthony with his stone-cold face. I found it so embarrassing how rude he would be to other men in hopes to communicate I was his.

When we exited the elevator and stepped into the rooftop restaurant, the bartender saw us both and waved. "Anthony, my man, come on over. Let me buy you and your beautiful fiancé a drink," he shouted over the loud music.

Anthony was well liked by the people who knew him; it was strangers who he was arrogant and rude to.

"Hey, man," Anthony said, giving the bartender a man hug.

"Good to see you. Give us two of your best glasses of Cab please. My princess loves her wine," he said, being sweet while making a subtle jab at my drinking.

I rolled my eyes and smiled at the bartender. "Yeah, whatever. I'm going to run to the ladies' room," I said and kissed Anthony on the cheek. As I walked away, I could feel his eyes watching me like a *hawk. I thought I'd be used to it after being engaged for a year and so close to our wedding, but it was the exact opposite. I felt more and more controlled by him, like I was a piece of property who no longer had a voice. Deep down, I knew Anthony loved me passionately and more than any guy I'd ever been with. Still somehow, our relationship felt more and more unsettling, like I was about to make one of the biggest mistakes, but I couldn't put my finger on why exactly.*

When I returned, Anthony was deep in conversation with the bartender about his business. I sipped my overpriced wine and looked around the room. The rooftop was beautiful, one of our favorite spots. I loved seeing the Chicago skyline with all its lights and hearing the excitement of the city. Since I was a teenager, I'd wanted to live in a big city with luxuries like this rooftop restaurant, a place where you felt like a somebody. I'd finally gotten that part of my life I'd always wanted.

Everywhere I looked there were beautiful people dressed to the nines. The women were skinny and fit—you could tell they took good care of themselves. Most of them wore bold fashions, loud shoes, and big jewelry with their hair and makeup done. They looked so confident and sexy, as though they had it all figured out. The men wore sport jackets, slicked-back hair, fancy shoes, and big watches like time was valuable. There were so many good-looking guys, but many of them had a subtle arrogance that wasn't attractive. The women laughed while sipping their martinis or vodka sodas with lemon, talking in groups with other beautiful people. I was envious of the women who seemed to be so confident, carefree, and alive. I thought, "I must be missing something because I didn't feel that same confidence and freedom." I second-guessed myself and my desires all the time. I wanted to feel more fulfilled, connected and empowered like these women. I bet they didn't tolerate a man being controlling or overly jealous. I bet they'd put Anthony in his place instead of just taking it like a weak and fearful woman. I didn't understand why I didn't feel more confident because I had almost everything I'd ever dreamed of: a gorgeous city-life apartment, a handsome fiancé, a fun job, nice clothes, and a great social life. Somehow, I still felt lonely, empty, and trapped. I questioned, "Is this all there is to life?" It left me longing for more. "When did I start feeling this way?" I wondered.

Wanting to speed our dinner up so I could get home, I said sternly, "Anthony, I'm hungry, let's go to our table," interrupting his conversation with the bartender.

"Yeah, yeah, Princess. I'll meet you over there," he said, smacking my butt. I could feel my face get hot with embarrassment—I hated when he did that in public.

I left to walk over to our reserved table, and as I did, I passed a table of four great-looking guys. One guy locked eyes with me and smiled. My stomach flooded with excitement followed by nervousness of what Anthony would do if this guy hit on me. Still feeling angry at Anthony, I chose to engage with an inviting half-smile.

"I think I've seen you here before. What's your name?" he asked, putting his napkin on the table, standing up and walking toward me.

My stomach dropped. I hadn't expected this guy to actually come toward me. If Anthony saw this guy talking to me, his reaction would not be subtle. I didn't want to be rude to the poor guy, but knew I had little time before Anthony spotted him making a move.

"I come here with my fiancé once a week. I'm sure you've seen us before," I said, quickly stating that I was taken, as though my ring didn't say it.

I heard Anthony walking up behind me. "Hey, man, I'm not sure why you're talking to my girl. Clearly, she's not interested in you, and she's wearing a ring you couldn't afford to give her," he said, grabbing my hand and holding it up in the guy's face.

I yanked my hand out of Anthony's grip and brushed him off. "Everything is clearly fine. I'll be at our table when you want to be a gentleman," I said, staring Anthony in his eyes.

"You don't deserve a woman like that, bro," the guy said as we walked away.

Something inside of me completely agreed with this stranger. I wondered why was I going to marry Anthony if I felt this controlled and angry half the time?

Our dinner was awkwardly quiet, and I kept drinking wine until I was so tired that I could barely hold my eyes open. It was how I ended half of our dinners when Anthony got jealous like that. It was easier to numb my anger, loneliness, and frustration than try to resolve any of our conflicts.

"He's just a really passionate guy. He loves me a lot," I was explaining to Sunny when she came out to visit.

"I know, Whit, but are you sure you want to deal with that for the rest of your life?" she asked. Sunny liked Anthony as a person but didn't like us together. She'd seen me in my other relationships and witnessed how dysfunctional most of them were. She knew I was repeating that.

"What if she's right?" I thought. Maybe I was about to marry a man who'd eventually get abusive with me, like my dad got with my mom. I couldn't imagine Anthony doing that. I knew he loved me, but what if I was wrong? What if his anger fits on the wall turned into anger fits on me? I bottled those thoughts up and pushed them way down.

"It's too late now—we're engaged. I've gone too far," I'd rationalize in my head. After all, we had our entire wedding planned and paid for. It would be back in Colorado. We'd already visited the wedding venue out there, and it was breathtaking: beside a lake with a gorgeous mountain backdrop. It was going to be in the fall with the leaves turning. I'd already bought and altered my dress. Everything was done.

There was only one problem: my bottled-up thoughts were becoming louder and louder. Our fights were getting more frequent and intense. I didn't know if I was instigating them by being more impatient with him, or if he was more comfortable fighting with me.

Either way, I felt a strong uneasiness about spending the rest of our lives together.

I fantasized about marrying a guy who loved Jesus, who was attracted to me but confident without being threatened. A man who was kind and thoughtful to others. A man who listened to my emotional needs, supported me, but gave me space to be myself. A man I'd want to have a family with, creating a home more nurturing than my childhood one.

"Who was I kidding, though?" I thought. I'd already messed up so many times for a man like that to be attracted to someone like me. I barely even had a relationship with Jesus—I didn't count going to church once a month as a strong pursuit of Him. My fantasy of being with that caliber of a guy was long gone. Plus, I figured I would probably be a neglectful mom, and it'd be better to not risk it. Still, there were so many questions of whether I was making a mistake marrying Anthony. It dawned on me that maybe he questioned the same thing.

"Do you ever second guess marrying me? Like wonder if I'm the right one for you?" I asked, hoping he'd be open to a real and honest conversation. We were in the kitchen cooking dinner together, sipping on some Cabernet, listening to music. I assumed the mood was just right.

He froze, turned around, paused for a moment, like he was pondering something, then stared me straight in the eyes. "Why are you second guessing, Whitney? Do you understand that this is no time for those type of ridiculous questions. My parents are flying all the way from Venezuela. It's three months away, and you're going to be stupid like that? Don't you dare take this away from me!" He yelled, slamming his fist on the countertop.

I was somewhat shocked by his response, but I was used to his unpredictability. I didn't want to fight, so I didn't say anything, but knew I couldn't share any of my inner doubts. I had to figure this out on my own.

Over the next few days, I obsessively went back and forth on how I envisioned my future. Was Anthony really the one or was I settling out of fear? "Of course he is, or I wouldn't be engaged to him," I'd think. "I know he loves me and I'm pretty sure I love him too. Plus, I'd miss him if we didn't get married and couldn't imagine another woman with him. Maybe I just need to fall back in love with him. Maybe I'm the problem, and our fighting is my fault. I bet we're both just under a lot of stress from all the wedding planning."

Later that week while he was at work, I was taking a shower when suddenly, it was like a wave of emotion came over me, and I burst into tears. My entire body weakened, and I fell to the floor sobbing. For the first time in years, I cried out, "God, I need You. Help me, I'm so scared. Please save me from this mess I got myself in!"

Something inside of me shifted—a conviction that was undeniable and so clear. I instantly knew I couldn't marry Anthony, I had to cancel our wedding, and there was no more second guessing. More importantly I need to pack my things from our place and leave as fast as possible. He wasn't going to take this news well, and I didn't want to stick around to see how he'd react.

"Mom, I'm calling off the wedding. I feel awful because we've spent tens of thousands of dollars and people already bought tickets, but something inside of me is saying I can't go through with this," I said, weeping over the phone.

My mom knew about some of the fighting we did, but she wasn't fully aware of just how often we fought or how jealous he really was. It wasn't all his fault. I knew I deserved his outbursts many times, but I didn't want her to know all that. Although deep down inside of me, I figured somehow she knew.

"It's okay, Sweetheart. You've got to listen to your gut. Don't worry about the money; that's not a valid reason to get married. Plus, you don't want a marriage with all that fighting—trust me. Pack what you can and come home." My mom's words were like water in a desert. They were exactly what I hoped to hear.

That night when Anthony left for work, I frantically shoved everything I could fit into the only three suitcases I had. I'd have to leave behind over half of my belongings from the last three years of living here, but I needed to get out and fast.

I wondered, "How did I get myself in this same position of fleeing again, leaving everything behind in an instant. What was I doing wrong?"

I came to Chicago several years ago to fix my life and start over. How was I leaving in worse condition than when I'd arrived? I thought, "God, if you haven't already abandoned me, you surely will now after these horrible mistakes and heartache disaster."

"Whit! Are you there?" Grace shouted, waving her hands in front of her face to get my attention.

A little embarrassed, not knowing how long I'd been staring off in space, I said, "Yes, I'm here. I apologize. I must be a little tired from all the shopping," I responded, trying to make light of the intense flashback I'd gotten caught in.

"It's not a problem at all, Whitney. We were just sharing how Gracie and I have been considering getting engaged in the next few months," Vincent said, gazing at Grace.

"Wow, I must have missed a lot," I responded, almost choking on my water. I looked at Grace—she looked blissfully happy but as though she were under a spell, too giddy. It reminded me how I felt when I'd first met Anthony, completely head over heels, infatuated with his good looks, money, and charm.

Grace looked at me. "Yes, Vincent started going to church on his own a few weeks ago, and I've just loved how he's so willing to pursue Jesus. When we first started dating, I told him my relationship with Jesus was important, but it took some time for him to come around on his own. I'm really proud of him." She turned to Vincent and kissed his cheek.

While I was relieved to hear about Vincent's faith, their relationship still had so many red flags. I wasn't sure how I'd tell Grace because it didn't seem like she was open to hearing feedback at all. To me, it seemed very clear—Grace had made up her mind that Vincent was her God's best.

"God, please give Grace the wisdom and discernment You gave me. Even when I was distant from You, I witnessed Your love pursue me amid my strongholds and blindness. It was all Your strength and courage that allowed me to break off my engagement to Anthony months before our fully paid for wedding. I know You can give Grace the same courage and wisdom to make the best decision," I prayed peacefully.

I refrained from asking too many more questions so we could finish dinner, and so Grace knew I loved and supported her no matter what. As they were finishing up their wine, and I was sipping decaf coffee, I felt the Holy Spirit nudge me to ask Vincent why He hadn't pursued Jesus before meeting Grace. Second guessing my nudge for a few seconds, I took the chance of Grace being uncomfortable by my question before ending our evening.

"Vincent, it's been a genuine honor getting to meet you briefly, and I can see Grace is very happy with you. Thank you for making the effort and taking out the time to do this. I'm sure I'll learn more about you as time goes on, but I am curious as to what prevented you from pursuing a relationship with Jesus before meeting Grace?" I softened my tone so there was kindness, instead of condemnation.

Vincent smiled quickly then his expression turned to a stone face. He looked out the window, took a deep breath. He seemed visibly annoyed by my question. "I'll give you a straightforward answer because I know how much Grace loves and adores you, but for most people this question is none of their business." Vincent's face flushed. "I came from a poor family, my parents divorced when I was young, and my mom was a single mom taking care of me and my siblings. Everything I have today—my businesses, wealth, and network—was built from my own blood, sweat, and tears. I wasn't handed one thing. I find it difficult to worship a God who is supposed to be good who allows fatherless kids to be raised by a struggling single mom and basically left to raise themselves from a young age. Now, I'm aware of the theology that says Jesus paid the price for our broken lives to put us back together, but I've been through too much and witnessed too many people I love suffering to easily surrender my entire life to a God who's supposed to be fully in control yet does so little to help the brokenhearted and oppressed." Vincent's voice had gotten a bit shaky, and I could sense that he was very passionate about this subject.

Although I could see his point of view and understood completely with my background and experiences, I sensed Vincent was nowhere near Grace's deep faith. It became glaringly obvious that Vincent and Grace were unevenly yoked, that their differences in faith, on their own journeys would become a huge point of tension if they got married. I could feel it so strongly. I took a sip of water to break the tension in the air, and I looked at Grace then back at Vincent.

Thankfully, our waiter appeared to ask if we needed anything else and drop off the bill. Vincent quickly grabbed the check before I could reach for it.

"Thank you, Vincent, for sharing your perspective and journey so far. I can see your passion, and I'm sure that's come with some pain. It's great to hear that you're maintaining an open heart to God." I didn't want to say much more or get into a deeper conversation about it because he didn't seem to be searching for answers but more concerned about defending his current state.

We walked out of the restaurant with a strange, awkward tension. I wasn't sure if I'd pushed too soon with the question, or if this was an experience Grace and Vincent had conversations about. Either way, I was happy to be heading to back to my hotel to bed. I was surprised at how emotionally exhausted I was even though it was so great to see Grace.

"Grace, let's set up a time to chat next week. It was so great to meet you, Vincent, and thank you so much for a generous and beautiful evening," I said, getting into my cab and blowing kisses.

Back at my hotel, I decided to walk around the neighborhood to get fresh air. It was cold, but the crisp air was refreshing with all the emotions I was experiencing with my burdensome flashbacks and my uneasiness about Grace's relationship.

"Jesus, I love You. You truly are my strength and my shield who saved me from self-destruction. When I was in distress, even though I wasn't pursuing You, You answered my cries of help. I'm so glad You gave me the courage and wisdom to break off my relationship with Anthony years ago. I would've been miserable and lonely. Jesus, I can tell there's still open wounds of shame from that experience, but You made me a new creation. Therefore, I'm not who my past says I am but who You say I am. Holy Spirit, come remove the shame from my mind, body, and spirit that is tied to my past with Anthony. Thank You for showing me that this was still rooted in me tonight. Thank You for Your unconditional love. Tonight, I declare I've received new healing," as I prayed that quietly, I felt a warm wave of peace wash over me. It gave me butterflies in my stomach and goosebumps all over my body. Then a second warm wave of peace washed over me, and this time my heart felt so tender I thought it might burst. I started weeping with gratitude for this loving encounter from the Holy Spirit. I'd experienced this a handful of times before, but it seemed a bit more intense and different. It felt like God was giving me an upgrade of joy by experiencing more of His goodness.

I woke up earlier than normal at 4:44 a.m. with Grace weighing on my heart. I wanted to decide how I'd tell Grace my thoughts about Vincent in the most loving way. I didn't think it'd be wise for her to get engaged to him—I didn't want her making the same mistake I had.

I sat down with coffee, my Bible, and journal and began to write whatever came to mind. I called it a brain dump, just clearing my mind by getting all the mind chatter onto paper. As I wrote, the tension became clearer. My past was haunting me, and the lies were coming on thick. Grace knew about my childhood trauma, some of my past rebellion, and a sprinkle of other events. "If she knew the whole truth like how much I'd partied with drugs and alcohol and how promiscuous I was, she'd never take advice from me. I've made so many mistakes, I shouldn't be mentoring anyone," I wrote.

As I was writing that out, I felt the Holy Spirit say, "My grace is sufficient for you, Whitney." A warm wave of relief washed over me. Tears came to my eyes, and my heart felt expansive. The Holy Spirit led me to Romans 11:6: "And since it is through God's kindness, then it is not by their good works. For in that case, God's grace would not be what it really is—free and undeserved." Then I flipped to 2 Corinthians 12:9: "Each time he said, 'My grace is all you need. My power works best in weakness.' So now I am glad to boast about my weaknesses, so that the power of Christ can work through me."

After reading both of those passages, I fell on my knees and thanked God for this incredible reminder that His grace is enough. My worth was based on God's goodness through Jesus's sacrifice, and now I am a *new* creature in Christ.

"I'm going to need to remind myself of these basic truths from God about *who* and *whose* I am for the rest of my life," I thought. I saw clearly how I still felt the need to strive, prove, and measure myself against others in fear of rejection or not being good enough. I felt the power of the Holy Spirit removing a layer of that orphan mindset. It was obvious to me now that the tension and heaviness I'd been experiencing this morning was an attack from Satan, tempting me to feel unworthy instead of using my testimony for wisdom and power. I spent the rest of my morning peacefully declaring God's promises over my life and Grace's life, praying that her eyes would be open to God's love for her, so she'd stop seeking it in guys.

*   *   *

I got back from Chicago and hit the ground running with work, holiday parties, and last-minute shopping. Before I knew it, Christmas had come and gone. It was a few days after Christmas that Grace texted me while I was at lunch with a coaching client, Jess. I hadn't seen Grace since Chicago, so I was grateful to hear from her.

"How is Grace doing?" Jess asked. I'd been coaching her for two years now and talked about Grace as a testimony several times.

"She's doing great except for the guy she's dating. It's wild how much she reminds me of myself—she tends to learn lessons the hard way. I'm concerned she's going to make the same mistake I did by saying *yes* to a guy who doesn't love Jesus like she does." I inhaled deeply, reminding myself that everything would be okay and that she was on her own journey with God.

"Have you told her what you think of this guy? You know she values your opinion so much. She's looked up to you for years now." Jess smiled. She knew she was right and was only reminding me of what I knew too.

Grace was in town for a few nights before flying to New York. I invited her over for dinner so we could catch up and I could hopefully bring Vincent up without her getting defensive or angry. She was coachable for 90 percent of our conversations; the other 10 percent was when we talked about guys.

Grace came over with a bouquet of flowers, a handwritten card, and homemade brownies. She was so thoughtful and charming—I loved that about her. As I finished cooking, I prayed inwardly, "Holy Spirit, I'm relying on You, not me, to convict Grace. Give me the words and unconditional love to talk to her about Vincent. I have a feeling it's going to be a hard conversation."

"So, Grace, tell me about meeting Vincent's family and spending Christmas with them." I expected to see her excitement bubbling over, but to my surprise that's not what I saw.

She stopped putting the flowers in a vase as though my question caught her off guard.

"Well, it wasn't what I expected," she said, turning toward me with tears in her eyes.

"Oh, I'm sorry. What happened?" I asked, now feeling concerned and overtaken by my curiosity of what she meant. I wondered if she was implying it was good or if I should be bracing myself for something difficult.

"They were amazing—so warm and welcoming. The first day, they wanted to take me shopping and go to my favorite restaurant. I can't explain how over the top they were in enthusiasm. Vincent's stepdad, who's very successful in his own business, was really sweet to me, and his mother was a very strong woman. I could tell she didn't just accept any girl into her son's life, but she absolutely adored me. But…" Grace paused again, tears falling down her cheeks. "Whitney, I don't think Vincent is my God's best, and as I say those words out loud it seems absolutely crazy. Honestly, I don't quite understand it. There's just something inside of me that says he isn't the one. I spent the last two days talking to Jesus about it, trying to make sense of the uneasiness I feel. That probably sounds crazy and so heartless, right?" She was fully crying now.

I was shocked in the best way, the conversation I was dreading was something I hadn't had to bring up. I walked over to her, put my arms around her, and ran my hand through her hair.

"Grace, that doesn't sound crazy at all, and I'm sorry. That's got to be hard," I said, doing my best to not share my previous revelation and be present with her. I knew just listening was what she needed in this moment.

"I just always imagined that when I met my God's Best he would be leading us in prayer, seeking Jesus on his own through devotions, and wanting to volunteer at the church we go to. That may seem a bit far-fetched, but I feel in my heart that my God's Best is a guy who desires a rich relationship with Jesus, and it's evident through his actions. It seemed like Vincent only pursued a relationship with Jesus when I brought it up. He felt annoyed when I asked him to volunteer at church, and when he did, he used it to flaunt what he'd done."

For the next two hours she shared all the untold details of how she hoped he'd love Jesus because she did and how they'd gotten into several arguments about faith, and that after meeting me in Chicago she saw more of his arrogant side. I was amazed at how similar our experiences were, just with a fifteen-year age gap. Grace being in my life felt like God smiling down on me. I felt so much gratitude for meeting her and Vincent in Chicago but more grateful that she concluded on her own that he wasn't her God's best, and she broke it off.

CONSIDER THIS

When will you stop running? When will you stop panting after other gods? But you say, "Save your breath. I'm in love with these foreign gods, and I can't stop loving them now!" (Jer. 2:25)

For me, I was running from my inner pain, shame, and unworthiness and then chasing after the false gods of this world, hoping they'd quench my thirsty soul. I didn't know it at the time because I was blinded by lies, haunted by unforgiveness, and enslaved to my passions.

What took me out of that muddy pig pen—which I needed multiple times—was calling on the name of Jesus. It was getting to the end of myself, from despair and defeat, that I'd call out to God, and Jesus would meet me in the middle of my messes, never judging or condemning me, always so compassionate and forgiving.

Ask the Holy Spirit, "Have I been running from things that You want me to face?" Let the Holy Spirit gently reveal parts of your heart that may need to be uncovered. When we leave these parts of our heart cold, hardened, or still wounded, we're more vulnerable to chasing after false gods, empty promises, and striving in the wind. The end of that road is lonely and oppressive. It doesn't lead to God's goodness because that's not where He is. The good news is that Jesus made a way for us to turn to Him at any point, so we can be free from our mistakes and messes.

CHAPTER FIVE

Saying "Yes"

I DIDN'T SEE GRACE FOR several months after she broke things off with Vincent. We'd text off and on, but she seemed more preoccupied than ever before, so I decided to let her reach out to me when she felt the need. I never stopped talking to God about her—it felt like the best way I could love her from afar. At times, I caught myself worrying about her, remembering how horrible of a shape I was in, emotionally, after I broke off my engagement with Anthony. Then I'd redirect my thoughts to God being the perfect Dad and the One who'd take care of her.

After fleeing from Chicago, I had moved in with my parents in Colorado for about a week before I realized there was no way I'd be able to live with them and stay sane. Inspired to someday own a business, I googled, "Best cities to start a business" and sure enough Austin, Texas, popped up as number one, so that's where I moved.

I'd love to tell you that after fleeing from Anthony that I learned my lessons, stopped creating messes, and pursued Jesus passionately, but that wasn't my case. I'd love to say it only required a few more years of heartache, but that also wasn't my case. There were many more late-night parties, guilt-filled days, and boys I kissed who I don't remember, which was the driving motivation for my next move (literally). I was bartending at one of the newest bars on West Sixth, called Dogwood. A guy who was on the TV show *The Bachelor* co-owned the bar, which made it the most popular place to go, so we usually had a line out the door to get inside. It was tough to beat bartending as a way to make good and fast money.

However, I missed the celebrity-like status I had as a Chicago bartender. There the bouncers listened to us on whom to let in and whom to kick out. On the busy nights in the three-story bar I worked in, if I didn't like you because you were rude or something, then you didn't get served. I had a regular following of people who'd come in to see me. In Chicago, I was the talent, but in Austin, I was the labor. The bar owners expected you to work longer hours, stocking your own beer, washing your own glasses. At the end of a long twelve-hour shift, we'd then have to clean the bar mats and wash the floors. It was an exhausting job that was more about the customer than it was about the bartenders.

"Hey, Sweetheart, I need another Miller Light," a guy yelled from the other side of the bar. I had my hands full, bent over one of the coolers grabbing beers for another customer, thinking, "Surely, this rude dude isn't talking to me because I hate being called *sweetheart*."

When I turned around, to my surprise, this guy was about six foot three with a pearl white smile, handsome, and just from glancing at him had *fun* written all over him. We ended up flirting the rest of the night. As I worked serving drinks behind the bar, he kept me busy making me laugh with his goofy but confident personality. There was something about this guy that I was so drawn to but knew I needed to be careful because it'd been less than one month since I'd broken off my engagement with Anthony. I knew I wasn't ready for any type of relationship.

That night I hopped on a rollercoaster from the pit of hell, and I didn't even realize how I got on or how to get off. McCaleb was the first guy I'd ever been with that I could have sworn an oath that we both agreed and knew we were just "having fun" together, nothing serious. He was a successful car salesman who knew everyone in the downtown Austin area and was known for partying hard and getting his way. It happened faster than I realized, but without knowing it, McCaleb fell head over heels for me. We'd only been hanging out for a few months, so I didn't take him seriously when he talked to other people about me being *his* girl.

One Friday night, I was slammed with people at the bar when McCaleb came over and slurred, "Babe, you need to come home with me right now!" He walked behind the bar and grabbed my arm like he was escorting me out. I got so embarrassed, I shrugged him off and signaled for the bouncer to come get him out. He punched the bouncer, then came back after me, "Babe, you heard me, let's go!"

"McCaleb, I'm not your babe, and you need to go home before I call the cops," I threatened, realizing how intoxicated and drugged up he was. This was the end of our relationship and the beginning of two consecutive months of him calling my phone at all hours of the night leaving voicemails threatening to kill my family and me. He'd leave notes on my car harassing and warning any guy who talked to me. It was a waking nightmare.

Eventually, one of my guy friends knew a private detective and told him about my situation. The detective visited McCaleb at the car dealership where he worked to make sure he got the message loud and clear to stop harassing me or he'd have him arrested. That was the last time I saw or heard from McCaleb.

I was relieved that I didn't have to deal with that frightening situation anymore, but there was still something inside of me that craved attention. A few more months went by since I'd called off the engagement, and I didn't feel any more relief. It was like there was a big void inside that I couldn't fill. The more I tried to make it go away, the more reckless decisions I made. All I could think about was meeting guys who drove fast cars or motorcycles and having fun drinking. It consumed my mind, and I couldn't get enough. I could feel my heart growing cold. I was purely chasing my own desires and didn't care who I hurt along the way.

A guy I met at a high-end cocktail party felt challenged by my "I don't care about you" attitude. He took my uninterested persona as an invitation to win me over in front of his friends. When I learned he drove a Lamborghini, my love for fast cars turned my "I don't care" attitude into an "I'm totally into you" attitude. That night, he had the guts or ignorance to let me drive his car. I fearlessly got it up to 113 miles an hour driving on the Texas Hill Country roads. It was incredible! Meeting all these successful guys in Austin, riding in fast cars, and partying with the "somebodies" was fun but surprisingly still not filling my inner void. In the quiet times at home, I felt lonely, worthless, and generally hopeless about ever fulfilling any purpose in my life.

In that moment, I got a call from my sister. "Whit, I want you to stay with me in Houston. The church I'm going to is incredible. It's a church plant, and I've been asked to be a leader for their welcoming team. We could really use the help. How about you come down next week and check it out?"

Sunny had lived with me in Chicago for a bit several years back and had gone through a big life change while I was now rebelling to avoid my inner pain. Her faith in Jesus was the strongest I'd ever seen it. I was happy to see her pursuing Him the way I craved but couldn't seem to execute. She was always there for me through the chaos, and at times my partner in crime, so I agreed to visit.

I was desperate for change. I knew if I kept going down the path I was going, I'd be back in the same exact position of running from a bad relationship or worse. That next Sunday, I drove to Houston for their church service. It was in an older, kind of run-down middle school. There were only about twenty members, including the small volunteer staff. I met the pastor and his wife, who were a few years younger than I was with a strong fire for Jesus. While being there, I instantly felt pulled to help with establishing and growing the church. Their church motto was simple: "Love God. Love People." I wondered if maybe I'd find the purpose I'd been missing.

"Sis, do you think if I moved here to help the church, the Lord would provide a job and place to stay?" I asked doubtfully. I hadn't ever trusted God in such a bold way before. I'd heard other people do it, but I certainly wasn't "holy" enough for God to provide for me in that way.

"Yes, I know an older couple you can stay with. I already asked them, in hopes you'd want to. They are helping with the church plant as financial supporters for what we're doing. They're a bit strict, but it'd probably be a good balance for you. That'll give you some rent-free time to find a job."

It sounded pretty good, and she was very convincing. Or maybe I was just ready to run again and subtly looking for an excuse. Either way, I was in.

*   *   *

Planting a church is hard work. We had to set up everything from a trailer, and at the end of a long night, we had to take everything down. It was fun, and the relationships we had were strong. We were all on fire to bring Jesus to this community, but it didn't take long before I was craving my old ways.

It may surprise you, but I hadn't thought this move all the way through. We were in a suburb of Houston, about forty-five minutes from the city. There was one grungy, small bar in town, definitely no night clubs to dance at, lame corporate restaurants, and definitely no opportunities to drive rich guys' Lamborghinis 113 mph at fancy cocktail parties.

"Ugh, what did I get myself into?" I thought as I lay in bed staring at the ceiling. This was the first time in almost a decade that I'd been away from partying regularly and getting my validation from men. I was bored out of my mind with strong urges to drink and meet others who also enjoyed drinking and having fun. It'd only been three months into this church plant, and I was second guessing the move.

"Who am I kidding? I'm not a church girl. If they knew about my past, they wouldn't allow me to be a leader of their welcome team. I'm basically lying to everyone here." These thoughts swirled in my head, and I was feeling anxious.

Everyone I'd become friends with was nice and welcoming, but we didn't have anything in common other than Jesus. When they told me about their struggles or past sins, I'd have to do my best to not laugh, thinking, "You call kissing a boy for too long one night a sin?"

There was a lot of inner turmoil. I was still talking to an old boyfriend back in Austin who I knew wasn't good for me. He loved to party more than I did, and we weren't good influences on each other. He was funny though and kept me company when I was lonely, so I kept him straggling along. I didn't consider him a prospect because I never gave him my heart and knew we were just a fling, but that didn't mean there wasn't some good ol' heartbreak coming his way from this one.

Sunny and I got together on Thursday nights to watch some cheesy TV show, drink a bottle or two of wine, and talk candidly about how different our lives were now.

"Sis, I've been in this boring suburb for six months now and still don't feel like Jesus is doing anything in my life. I feel silly living out here. I'm in my late twenties and don't even have my own place. Plus, most people at our church are younger than me and already married with kids. Their lives are more together than mine. I just don't belong," I vented as I sipped my wine.

"I understand, but the people love you here. You have so much to offer with your wisdom," she said, gently putting her hand on my shoulder.

I laughed, almost spitting out my wine. "When you say *wisdom*, what you really mean is I can tell them what *not* to do, as evidenced by a life of bad choices," I said judgmentally but in full belief that it was the obvious truth to everyone else too. I was one of the oldest church planters, and I was single with no career. However, I was grateful to be closer to Sunny. It felt good to have her here to talk to, and I knew she loved me despite my craziness.

That Sunday the pastor's wife came up to me, "Hey, Whitney, I remembered you saying you'd love to get baptized if we ever offered it as a church. We're going to do our first baptism in a few weeks, and I wanted to personally tell you." She was one of the most genuine and down-to-earth women I'd met. I never felt judged by her even though we had nothing in common other than we both openly doubted our worthiness and knew we needed Jesus's love.

"Oh, that'd be great! Do you need me to be a leader at it, or is it okay that I get baptized?" I asked, hoping she'd say they needed my help, and I'd get out of the baptism. (I didn't remember saying that I wanted to get baptized, but I'm sure I did at some point.)

"Nope. Girl, we've got you. I'm so excited." She gave me a big hug then walked away.

I was nervous the day of my baptism. It was an outside sign that I wanted to live my life for Jesus, but truthfully, I'd wanted to live for Jesus since my seventh-grade year, and twelve years later I hadn't represented my friend Jesus well at all. I was pretty sure He was embarrassed by me, and that I'd be doing Him a bigger favor by *not* outwardly saying, "I follow Him."

That day, a group of five or six of us, including me, got baptized in a church elder's backyard pool. While I waited, watching others give their life openly to Jesus and listening to their testimonies, I was doubtful that I'd be able to live up to my proclamation of following Jesus. My record wasn't a good one.

"Whitney, you're next," the pastor said, waving me down into the water where he was standing. Sunny grabbed my hand and walked with me to assist him.

I listened to him read the testimony I'd written. My eyes welled up with tears, and my heart felt full. This was who I wanted to be—someone who loved Jesus. I just hoped I'd be able to do it.

He finished reading my testimony, said a prayer, then gently baptized me under water. When I came up for breath, I literally felt like new life breathed into me. I was lighter. My body felt tingly all over. There was a new sense of joy in my soul I hadn't ever experienced. I didn't know if others baptism experience were like this, but I was instantly grateful that I said *yes* to giving my life to Jesus. "Maybe God had been with me this entire time," I thought.

*   *   *

Moving to help the church plant and getting baptized were two events where I was saying *yes* to God's purpose and calling. Most of my life, I was running the show, then asking Him to either *bless it* or *save me*. Both the church plant and getting baptized felt scary with so many unknowns. But I began to build spiritual muscle—a personal relationship with Jesus and the Holy Spirit like I'd never had before. It was creating a bigger hunger for more of this God-focused living. I had less desire to chase after the things of this world. It made sense why God pulled me out of the city living and into the suburbs, so He could deal with some old heart wounds, and I wouldn't be constantly tempted to fall back into old patterns. He wanted to take me somewhere I could rest, heal, and focus on Him.

Even though I could see a light at the end of the tunnel, the shame still felt heavy day to day, constantly reminding me of my past. I was ashamed that I hadn't waited for my future husband, that I partied too much, that I broke a lot of hearts, that I ran from my problems, and drank until I was numb. My childhood made me feel even more broken. All that baggage felt so heavy, but I didn't know how to let it go.

Looking back I see that what I was experiencing was exactly what happens when you say "yes" to adventure with God before you feel capable. It's a lifestyle I value but at the time, I'd never done it before, it felt so incredibly uncomfortable that I assumed I was being reckless again. My heart was being positioned to have the adventure centered on Jesus instead of my own passions of the world. The process of that transition looked messy, but God's grace is so much bigger.

*   *   *

God created you with a beautiful and amazing purpose. The enemy wants nothing more than to see you give up on the goodness God has in store for you and give up on what He wants to do through you. There is no one on this planet like you: experience, talent, personality, and DNA. We've got to believe this, no matter what we've done, gone through, or have had done to us.

CONSIDER THIS

Faith shows the reality of what we hope for; it is the evidence of things we cannot see. (Heb. 11:1)

What are you being called to say *yes* to that's going to require you to have faith? Is it a dream or goal you've had for years that you've given up on? Maybe it's a purpose that just doesn't seem like it's "the right time," and you keep pushing it on the back burner. The courageous experience of saying *yes*, then committing to the journey is worth it for the deeper faith and character development alone. When you commit to one step at a time, you're never too old or too far away from pursuing your next *yes*. The key is to do it with Him by keeping your eyes on Him. God is limitless, loves to do the impossible, and keeps dreaming with His children—it's who He is, and He designed us for that, too. When we stop adventuring with God, we start dying from the inside.

Life is meant to be your greatest adventure and will require you to keep renewing your mind to uproot the lies that cause fear and doubt so you can see more from His perspective than from your limited and small view.

I diligently guard and protect my mind and heart each day so I can keep moving forward with Him by faith. Many of the dreams I have on my heart today I don't see, so I have to take steps without seeing the evidence of it working. I make it a habit to proactively renew my mind, an offensive strategy I have in play to deepen my faith. I want to be mentally, spiritually, and physically fit so I can handle whatever comes my way and be hopeful about the future God has in store. When I miss a day of renewal, I pick right back up on guarding, equipping, and renewing my mind with God.

Doubt is going to come up. It's part of the human experience, but you don't want doubt to be your decision maker. That's one of the obstacles that keeps you thinking small, putting limitations on God, and chasing the wrong things. Thankfully, God loves you so much, His grace is bigger than our kindergartener-like attitudes. He meets us where we are, gives us opportunities to mature, and then invites us again to adventure with Him.

Ask the Holy Spirit, "What are you calling me to that I've been avoiding or too fearful of?" Spend some time journaling whatever comes to your mind. Then imagine, what if you said *yes* to your next God-given adventure, how would that positively impact your life?

CHAPTER SIX

Don't Quit

I COULDN'T EVEN REMEMBER WHEN I last spoke to Grace, which I didn't like, so I decided to give her a call. Thankfully, she answered. She was driving to go snowboarding, so we had some time to catch up. She shared how she'd been a little worried about how often she was drinking but assured me she was fine and to not worry about her. I was grateful for her honesty.

"Grace, is there something you're avoiding? In the past I know when I've turned to drinking more frequently, I was avoiding some internal pain, shame, or self-hatred. Do you have any of that coming up?" I asked.

I could hear her tearing up over the phone.

"Yeah, I just keep trying to find my sense of security and worth from guys. I've been inviting Jesus into my pain, but then it's like I forget and go back to old patterns. Will I ever get to a point where I'm living *from* Jesus's love not *for* His love?"

"Oh, Grace, you will definitely get past that. My guess is that Jesus is just calling you deeper into healing. Let me tell you another story of when I was learning the lesson, yet again, after so many failed attempts and being miserable," I said with compassion and light-heartedness before filing her in.

* * *

Single and still not meeting any potential-husband candidates in the suburbs, I'd frequent happy hours downtown during the week. That's when I met Nate, a big, tall guy who looked like a football player but who had played lacrosse in college. An investment banker who had previously lived several years in New York and moved to Houston to get out of the fast-paced life, he was raised a southern boy who loved fishing, hunting, big trucks, and country music. Unfortunately, that included strip clubs with work buddies and a view of women I didn't care for. I vocalized my distaste for it, but he didn't see a problem with it.

We met at a happy hour where we enjoyed a few glasses of wine together and spent an entire evening talking and laughing. He asked the waiter to upgrade the wine I was drinking, but I didn't feel any strings attached to his generosity, which was refreshing.

He seemed well-established, responsible, and a true southern gentleman, all quite different from anyone I'd ever dated. He traveled quite a bit for work (back and forth to New York or Los Angeles) and worked twelve to fourteen hours a day, but I liked that he was a hard worker focused on his career. His job was high stress, and he was constantly tied to his phone checking emails and responding.

Because his career came first, our relationship consisted mostly of weekends spent together. We'd go out for fancy steak or to Italian restaurants, which often included bottles of $100 wines. I'd be his date for work or charity events he attended. At times, I felt like his "arm charm," only there because I was easy on the eyes. At these events, he'd have work or sophisticated conversations that bored me, and I'd usually tune them out and frequent the bar. I had zero desire to impress the people around him. I think that's one of the things he liked about me—I was independent and didn't care what his friends or coworkers thought about me.

Ours was a fun lifestyle and relationship. I loved the fancy dinners, social scene, and getting the five-star treatment everywhere we went. Somehow, I still felt lonely. I didn't feel emotionally connected but just assumed it was because our intellectual interests were different. Our lack of emotional connection didn't seem to bother him though. I started to wonder if this was the best I'd find. He took good care of me, always being generous with zero manipulation, treating me with respect for the most part, and wanting the best for me. I was grateful for those parts of our relationship.

Six months in, he asked, "Wanna fly to NYC with me next week? I have to work a few days. On Friday we'll drive to my beach house in Cape Cod. Don't worry about money—I'll pay for everything. Plus, I have plenty of air miles that I need to use." He reassured me the trip would be covered.

The trip seemed like a necessary next step in our relationship, but I might have been falling for the luxurious lifestyle we had more than falling for him.

"Yes, let's do it!" I said, excited and nervous about how this trip would affect our relationship. I didn't want to get into another serious relationship unless I was certain he was "the one." The biggest conflict in our relationship so far had been that he didn't feel a need to pursue Jesus on his own beyond us attending church. It seemed very similar to my broken engagement with Anthony.

We ended up having a blast together! We stayed in a cute boutique hotel a few blocks from the stock exchange where his office was. While he worked, I window shopped. His beach house in Cape Cod was an older house that he had bought to remodel. It was super cute, and we saw lots of potential in it. We sipped mai tais, ate fresh oysters, danced, and watched the sunset on a beautiful boat dock. It was a slice of heaven.

It was the first of several fancy trips we took together. It was fun, but as our relationship was getting more and more serious my doubts were growing stronger.

*   *   *

It was Thursday, my sister date with Sunny. Most of the time, we kept conversation light and fun, but tonight was different. She asked some painfully tough questions that caught me off guard. "Whit, when are you going to stop leading him on?" she boldly asked, giving me a side stare that felt very convicting like I'd just gotten caught doing something bad.

"What are you talking about? I'm not leading him on. I really do like him. Plus, he's the best guy I've dated since Anthony. We don't fight near as bad as my previous relationships." I felt judged and unfairly called out.

She rolled her eyes, took a sip of her wine, then topped off our glasses. She knew he didn't have a personal relationship with Jesus, and she saw how much time we were spending together. I knew exactly her point—I was making the same mistake I had made with Anthony, staying in the relationship for this new lifestyle and financial security.

"He doesn't love Jesus like you do. You've made some hard changes in your life to put your faith first, and he doesn't see it as important. He's going to end up proposing, and you're going to run because that's how you handle life. You'll break his heart, Whit," she said this time with more love and compassion.

I felt punched in the gut. It was too apparent to deny. I kept thinking, "I just need more time for him to see how having a faith in Jesus is important," but it'd already been over a year.

"So what should I do?" I asked with tears streaming down my face. I didn't want to hurt him any more than I knew I would at this point. Plus, I didn't want him to have to change for me or feel like he couldn't be himself.

"My honest answer? Don't go on your next Cape Cod trip with him and his family. You need to end it," she said, giving me a hug.

I felt a ton of guilt and shame. "I shouldn't have dated him in the first place. I keep making the same mistake over and over."

*   *   *

A few weeks passed, and I called Nate to see if he wanted to attend church with me, since we weren't already hanging out that night. I'd usually call the night before to invite him if he was working over the weekend. I enjoyed having his company and loved when we got dressed up for church, attended together, and usually ate at one of our favorite brunch places with a mimosa or two after.

"Hey, I'm going to church tomorrow at 8:45, the early service. Do you want to go? No pressure if you have to work late tonight and need more sleep," I said, not being fully honest. I didn't like when he'd choose work over going to church with me, but I also knew our luxurious lifestyle required him to work hard.

"I can't tomorrow. I've got a hard deadline with this company. I'll probably be up late tonight and have to fly to New York early Monday morning for a last-minute trip," he said with stress in his voice.

I knew his job required a lot of him, but I couldn't help my rising disappointment and frustration. "Sure. I'll talk to you next weekend then," I said trying to hide my emotion but also hoping he'd notice.

"Whit, I can tell you're mad. I don't know what to tell ya though," he said raising his voice.

I could feel my heart race and face get hot. Sunny's words to me a few weeks before rang loudly in my head: "You're leading him on. He isn't pursuing Jesus on his own. You're going to end up ending things with him and breaking his heart."

"Nate, I totally understand that your career comes first, but I feel like if it weren't for me asking if you wanted to attend church with me that you wouldn't ever go. It's frustrating that I'm constantly the one instigating, inviting, and encouraging you to grow your faith. You knew it was important to me when we first started seeing each other. It's fine. I get that you're stressed and working late, but you need to figure this out on your own. I'm sick of carrying us both. If you don't figure it out, then this needs to be the end of our relationship."

I couldn't believe all that came out. I didn't like threatening him that our relationship would end if he didn't pursue Jesus on his own, but I didn't know how else to make it clear that I was serious. On one hand, I feared losing him, the luxury, the travel, and the expensive gifts. On the other hand, I was more convinced that those things weren't worth my relationship with Jesus becoming lukewarm or feeling alone in my spirituality. I wanted a teammate who prayed with me, loved Jesus more than I did, and didn't need me to encourage that.

"Wow! My weekend just went to crap. Thanks, Whit! Now, I have stress about my job *and* losing my girlfriend. That's great. Well, I'm glad it's so easy for you to just let go of what we have. I'm not going to try to convince you that my love is enough because you obviously don't think that way. I want to be with you, Whit, but I can't handle this hot and cold over my faith journey and our relationship," his tone lowered with sadness.

I sensed his fear that I'd leave him, and I hated that I made him feel that way. I didn't want to hurt him, but my relationship with Jesus was something I wanted to prioritize more.

The next few nights I was unable to sleep, asking God what to do, praying for Nate to desire a personal relationship with Jesus. God showed me how it'd been an ongoing point of tension in our relationship for a while, but I had been refusing to see it as a problem and kept justifying it, hoping in time he'd change.

Fear washed over me. "God, I'm getting older, not younger, and the thought of starting all over in the dating process feels painful and hopeless. I'll probably never find a guy worth marrying. My standards must be too high. A girl like me has made too many mistakes to marry a God-fearing man like I'd hoped I would when I was a teenager," I prayed from desperation.

There was a real temptation to give up on that dream and settle for less than my vision.

But the more time I spent praying about it, the clearer it became that God was asking me not to quit on the vision. He was asking me to take a leap of faith and trust Him again. I felt it deep from within, even though I wondered if I was being wishful.

That week while Nate was traveling for work, I went on several walks at the park near my house to remember all the previous times when I trusted God and He hadn't let me down. Even when I'd felt hopeless, He'd show up in miraculous ways. I had truly witnessed over and over that God is worthy of trusting, even when I couldn't see how it would work. Since I had moved to Houston three years earlier to help plant the church and get baptized, my relationship with Jesus had reached new levels of healing and trust. I didn't want to lose that, and more importantly, the desire for more of Him was growing. I boldly decided I wasn't going to quit on finding a God-fearing man. I decided I'd rather live alone than in a relationship where we didn't share the same passion for Jesus.

Nate returned from his work trip and took Friday off to recover from an eighty-hour work week. He'd called to ask me over for dinner. He enjoyed grilling filet mignon for us and sipping on wine while he cooked.

I was 60 percent sure I needed to end it that evening. After praying and reflecting, I felt right in my spirit, but I was sad it wasn't ending differently. I wanted Nate to be the one so I could stop looking, but I wasn't ready to give up on what I felt God was calling me to.

We grilled on his patio, listening to country music, sipping wine, and joking around. Nate was in an unusually good mood, which made the night feel harder. I knew I should have broken things off last weekend after our argument over the phone.

After finishing dinner, Nate pulled me close. "So I bought us tickets to Cape Cod, and my parents are meeting us out there. I think this is the trip we need. I know you were mad at me last weekend about church, but I know you're the girl for me, Whit. You're the only one I've dated who understands the stress of my career, encourages me to be a better man, and is patient with me."

My stomach dropped as I felt the tenderness of his heart.

I thought, "I can't tell him now. Maybe I should wait after our trip. I'm sure we'll get in some small argument, and it'd be easier to wait until that happens." Not knowing what to do, I prayed, "God, I want to pursue you over every other desire I have. You made it clear this past week that Nate isn't the one. I need Your courage, discipline, and help right now. This is hard." I set my wine glass down and faced Nate.

"Uh-oh, you look serious," he said, observing my posture and look on my face.

Tears welled up in my eyes, and I tried to hold them back and stop from crying before I got the words out of my mouth. "Nate, you deserve better than me. It's not fair to you that I'm asking you to rush your faith journey and to be different than you are. I understand that your career is number one, and I don't want to change that for you. I also need a man who passionately pursues Jesus on his own. I've been putting that pressure on you since we started dating. It's lonely to feel like I'm wanting more in my faith and you're not. We're just not in the same place of life. I can't keep going on these trips with you and getting more serious when I know deep down we aren't right for each other." Tears streamed down my face. I was trying hard not to take back what I was saying. We'd had conversations like this before, but this time felt final. I knew he wouldn't pursue us after tonight, and I knew it was the last straw.

Nate turned his face away.

I could feel the heaviness and tension. I knew if I stayed to comfort him it wouldn't help because this moment needed to be hard. It was the end. I grabbed his hand and kissed the top of it. "Nate, thank you for everything. You're an amazing guy, and I know God has a special woman for you. Goodbye," I said, getting up from the couch and walking myself to the door.

When I got to my car, I let out a loud sob. "Why God? Why do I keep learning the hard way? I'm an idiot. I hate that I just broke his heart and had to end something amazing. This is so painful!" I shouted.

I decided from that day on that before I go on any date, I'd ask about the guy's relationship with Jesus. If he didn't have one or if it seemed to be lukewarm, then we'd never go on a first date and our conversations ended right then. I was done dating to be busy. I was drawing a line in the sand. The pain felt so real; it was my final lesson.

Two weeks later, I packed up my bags and moved from my tiny apartment in the Houston suburb and back to Austin. I couldn't stay in the same city as Nate because it felt too small, and we had so many shared memories. After breaking up with him, I felt like I hit my rock bottom, struggling emotionally, feeling lost and hopeless. I moved in with Brooke and Henry, didn't have a job, and had $500 to my name. I no longer could afford those fancy dinners I was fond of; heck I couldn't even afford Whataburger. I missed being wined and dined, and even with the loneliness of my last relationship, I still missed having someone to talk to.

I wanted to quit on my dreams of marrying a God-fearing man, impacting the world, and being a business owner. I wanted to throw in the towel. "You need to dream more realistically, Whit. What you are trusting God for isn't going to happen or it would have already happened by now," I thought. This doubt would play over and over in my head, creating more worry.

Even though those lies felt so real, there was something inside of me, a hunger for more that wouldn't allow me to completely give up. A deep desire kept pushing me forward, believing for a bigger life, and trusting God that things would get better. Most of my friends from high school and from other places were already married with kids. I believed I was royally messing my life up, but I kept desiring what I felt He was calling me to.

For the next several months, I went to a nearby Starbucks, used my credit card to buy a cup of black coffee that I couldn't afford, and journaled with God.

I'd write, "I'm married to a God-fearing man who pursues Jesus passionately on his own. He's an amazing teammate who honors and respects me. He's not jealous, controlling, or needy. He's confident but humble and knows how to make me laugh. We have a best-friend type of relationship, wanting to travel and dream big together. We live in a beautiful house. We own a business where my schedule is flexible, and I'm earning enough for our family to give generously on a regular basis. In my business I'm helping others overcome struggles that I've had breakthrough in. I'm finally on the other side of my hard lessons and healed from childhood trauma. I like who I am." I'd go on and on about this vision, imagining it, writing it, and then surrendering my heart desires over to God.

This frequent exercise of imagining my future and writing it on paper gave me a confident expectation that breakthrough was around the corner because of God's goodness and promises.

CONSIDER THIS

And this hope will not lead to disappointment. For we know how dearly God loves us, because he has given us the Holy Spirit to fill our hearts with His love. (Rom. 5:5)

Hope is the foundation for steadfastness. When you lose hope, your motivation and endurance go out the window too. This is why it's so important to keep our hope burning like a fire. You keep your hope alive by staying focused on God's goodness and His promises. The truth is that God loves you so much, He wants you to prosper, to live hope filled in every area: relationships, purpose, health, family, etc. When you prosper and lived blessed, then you get to be a testimony of His goodness and faithfulness.

Experiencing more of His love requires you to surrender, to stop striving in your own strength and self-will, so He can do the heavy lifting. It's honestly liberating—no more striving, pushing, and grinding through to try to make things work. Surrendering each area of your life to God is a faith-based but powerful way of living. It means to unclench your fists and live with an open hand. Surrendering all to God is saying, "He is my Source, not me." These are two Kingdom principles—trusting and surrendering.

It's easy to go to church each Sunday, make your plans, pursue your desires, and ask God to bless what you are doing. I lived that way for decades, and it leads to emptiness, but you are free to choose.

Ask the Holy Spirit, "What areas am I holding on to with a closed fist and need to surrender and trust God with?" Write down whatever comes up. I invite you to say this simple prayer:

Heavenly Father, help me to experience new revelations of Your love for me. I want to experience just how deep, wide, and good Your love for me is. Thank You for loving me so much that You sent Jesus, Your only Son, to pay the price for all my shame, guilt, and sin. I confess I've chased after things of this world more than I have You. I've been busy building my kingdom instead of living for Your heavenly Kingdom. Forgive me. I break agreement with this orphan way of thinking, lacking in love, trying to earn it. Today, I choose to surrender and trust in You in every area. Come now and do a new thing in my mind, heart, and body so I can experience more of Your love. In Jesus's Name. Amen.

CHAPTER SEVEN

Divine Calling

I 'D JUST FINISHED A TOUGH but energizing bootcamp class at my favorite gym, T3. I always felt stronger and more inspired after those classes. I grabbed a cup of coffee from the gym's coffee shop, said *hi* to a few friends, and then headed out to my car when my phone buzzed with a message from Grace: "Happy sobriety day! You are such an inspiration. Thanks for all your support. You're an amazing role model. I love you very much, Whit."

Tears welled up in my eyes. I'd forgotten it was my sobriety anniversary. This day had become more important to me than my birthday. I couldn't believe I'd forgotten.

"Thanks, Gracie! I'm incredibly grateful that you're in my life too. Let's schedule a time to catch up next week. Love you!"

Grace's mom was still struggling with choosing drinking over spending time with her. I knew Grace's appreciation for my life commitment came from painful experiences of knowing what it was like to have a parent who consistently choses alcohol. I knew her pain too well, and it was heartbreaking to watch.

I drove home, rolled the windows down, blasted worship music, sang, and thanked God out loud for His faithfulness. I was overjoyed not to be imprisoned by alcohol anymore, and my sobriety day was a special day when I got to acknowledge the power of it.

As I drove, I reflected on the path that led me to this life-altering decision. I recalled that I never used to think I had a problem with alcohol. I was never so dependent that I needed it when I woke up, and I'm sure this misconception prevented me from giving alcohol up sooner. "I'm not an alcoholic because I don't drink like that, so I'm sure I don't have a problem with drinking," I'd justify to myself.

My relationship with alcohol felt controlled, most of the time.

I lost count of how many times I'd tell myself I wasn't going to drink for thirty days, usually to try to lose weight, but without fail, a friend would call, "Whit, I've had a stressful week. I bought us a bottle of wine. Will you come over?" Of course I would because that's what good friends do, and of course we'd each finish a bottle of wine because if you opened one, then you couldn't waste any of it.

Sometimes when I did go over to a girlfriend's house for wine, we'd end up going to a local bar for more drinks—after all, we were single and wanting to just have fun. After nights like that, I'd wake up with a horrible headache and a heavy weight of guilt. "Did I say anything stupid?" I'd ask my friend. Most of the time I hadn't, but since I became more outgoing and feistier when I drank, it left me wondering.

The scariest part was at least once every few months I wouldn't remember how I'd gotten home. Those nights were the worse to wake up from. I'd end up in my bed wondering where I was. Most of the people I knew shared similar experiences though, which made me assume my relationship with alcohol was not problematic.

"Maybe I only need to drink two nights this week: Friday and Saturday."

"I think it's only white wine that causes me to have horrible headaches."

"If I give it up for Lent, then I'll know Jesus is still Lord over my life and alcohol."

"I bet it's just hard liquor that makes me act out. If I can just stick to wine, then I'll stay in control."

I'd tried new policies like this more times than I could count, usually after I'd gone a little too hard, like after a vacation or string of celebrations. When this happened, I felt bloated, foggy in my mind, and my anxiety levels were higher than usual. My common phrase was, "Oh, I'll get back on track on Monday."

When I looked around at my friends and family, my drinking didn't look much different from theirs, but there was something inside that was tormenting me. I knew God was calling me to more, and this conviction hurt so bad I kept numbing it. I'd go through seasons where I felt incredibly insecure and self-conscious unless I had a glass of wine to take off the edge. Once I did, I'd feel more normal again, the *relief* alcohol provided was usually only temporary. The more I drank to relax, the more I felt I needed it to relax. Internally, I knew this was a sign that I was using alcohol as an emotional crutch.

Finally, I decided to make a change the year after I broke up with Nate—it seemed as though I'd hit rock bottom. I was feeling so empty, anxious, fearful, and alone. I'd finally reached a breaking point. I didn't want to keep getting stuck in the same vicious cycles. It was hard for me to stay focused on God's purpose when I was consistently feeling guilt and a lack of hope. Alcohol had become a crutch, and I didn't want to keep getting the same defeating results. I was ready to change.

Plus, when I looked back on the last fifteen years, the common denominator of bad decision-making or regret was always alcohol. When I wasn't drinking, my behavior was more in line with who I wanted to be. Alcohol was the consistent factor in the messes I'd get myself in.

"God, I need your help. I want to stop drinking, but I don't know how. This feels extremely hard. I've already failed more times than I can count, but if You will use my current pain to help one person, then I'll take this journey with You, knowing it will all be worth it." I cried out to God on my knees next to my bed. I'd woken up with massive anxiety from drinking with friends the night before and knew today was the day I'd had enough.

A few days later, a group of us from church were at country dance bar. They were having a few drinks, and I was miserably drinking water when I noticed a new girl, Kate, was the only other one drinking soda water with lemon.

I noticed she still wasn't drinking when we both went up to order from the bartender. "You're not drinking anything else?" I asked. I assumed she was a designated driver for someone because I'd never met someone who didn't drink at all.

"Nope, I don't drink. I gave it up a year ago," she said with a smile.

I was shocked but knew right then that God had sent me a solution to my prayer.

Kate and I went to coffee later that week when she vulnerably shared how she had decided to give up alcohol after a handful of mistakes while drinking too much in school to become a nurse practitioner. She said the drinking was a stumbling block for the plans she knew God had for her. I could completely relate and envied her discipline and focus for God.

As Kate's and my friendship grew, I witnessed the freedom she lived in by not desiring to drink anymore. It was so inspiring to witness that I wanted what she had. She was confident and focused on meeting a God-fearing man. I wanted to be like that.

I kept remembering how, when I still lived in Houston and was doing a Beth Moore Bible study, I heard the Lord say, clear as day, "I want you to give up alcohol. I have a calling for you, and alcohol is holding you back from the life I want to give you."

Since I'd already tried hundreds of times to "cut back" permanently, I knew I needed to give it up completely. I was fully convinced it's what God wanted *for* me, not *from* me. Whatever was waiting for me on the other side of this sacrifice, I trusted it would be totally worth it.

I could see clearly that God put Kate in my life to help me. She'd gone through the process already. She was the same age and a social person like me. If she could do it, I thought, then I could. I wanted the freedom and confidence she had.

Those first months of not drinking were by far the hardest. My brain felt foggy, anxiety levels were constant, and new memories of heart wounds that I'd run from were popping up. The other hard part was being surrounded by people drinking everywhere I went, often times pressured or questioned "Why aren't you drinking? You should drink."

At the time, I worked at a young tech start-up company. Almost every Friday after five o'clock, the company had a keg of beer as a reward for the sales department. It seemed like not drinking was the "impossible diet." It wasn't very socially friendly. Even my church friends wanted to go to bars or drink during our dinners. I didn't want that to bother me, but I wasn't yet free from alcohol. I still desired the buzz and felt insecure in social settings.

Prior to this journey, I was blind to how much I relied on alcohol. It was incorporated in so much of my life: how I celebrated, relaxed, socialized, and loosened up. Since that's the way society was, it never dawned on me that it was a crutch. It's even how I witnessed my family doing life; I didn't know anything different. I believed my drinking was fine because I could go ten days or so without it. I justified that I enjoyed the taste, and of course, I loved the buzz, but I was in denial about how often I chased that buzz, always wanting more once I started. I'd never questioned it until the last few years of feeling so empty and alone no matter what I did.

In the first year, there were a handful of days I'd come home at five thirty with intense urges to drink. It usually happened after feeling pressure from my manager or when I'd received a phone call from my family sharing bad news about Dad. It would send me right back into childhood memories. I'd flashback and feel the same fear I felt as a little girl running from my dad to get help. The negative emotion happened so fast that instantly I'd have an urge to drink. "Just one drink—no one needs to know," I'd think. The mind chatter was so loud, I'd get anxious then frustrated with myself that I was even considering it as an option.

"You're so weak, Whitney. You're not strong enough to do this. It's only a matter of time before you cave," I'd argue in my head, feeling hopeless that the desire would ever leave.

Over time, God showed me that these urges to drink were open wounds that He wanted to heal. When I drank, I was so used to how it numbed my emotions that I didn't even know I felt sad or hurt. I had lost connection to my true emotions. There was no longer a way to even know myself.

* * *

Kate's and my apartment was across the street from the original Summer Moon Coffee shop, my favorite. We loved treating ourselves to coffee there. So I spent many Saturday mornings on their outdoor patio journaling. Next to eating sugar, journaling while drinking coffee was my other hobby.

To stay hopeful and focused, I'd read through my journal about the future vision I wanted so badly, even though it felt very far away. I was broke, barely paying rent, only seven months without drinking in this new life, and I had decided to stop dating guys so I could focus on Jesus healing my past wounds. There were zero prospects for a future husband, and my life felt boring from where I was sitting.

I imagined my life looking vastly different than it did. I'd write in my journal about the things I was proud of, to switch from feeling defeat to feeling encouraged. I was grateful for breaking off an engagement, helping a church plant, ending a serious relationship where Jesus wasn't the focus, and cutting out alcohol to pursue the path God was calling me to.

At the time, there was still no sign as to how I'd be helping people with my testimony of giving up alcohol, but when I looked back to all the times God was trustworthy, I trusted He would provide a way.

When I reflect on pieces of that journey, of becoming someone who no longer is controlled by alcohol, I'm incredibly grateful. I see people I love—family and friends—who aren't living in the freedom I've experienced, and it's hard to watch. I wish they could taste what I've experienced on the other side. I'm confident if they could, they'd never want to go back to alcohol. The liberation is literally priceless.

*   *   *

I was finally going on my first date after taking a seven-month break. A friend had talked me into signing up for a dating app, *OkCupid*. I wasn't super excited about being on a dating app; it seemed a bit extreme, but I felt hopeful that I was finally the woman I wanted to be for my future God's best. I had surrendered my desires to Jesus, I was living a sober life, and I was starting to like who I was.

I'd been on the app for a few days and gone on two horrible dates when I received a fun, personable, and genuine message from a guy named Jake. He commented on my surfing profile picture that I'd taken while visiting El Salvador just a few days prior. He called me "a Texas Surfer," which I loved hearing.

A few days later, on May 30, 2016, we went on our first date. We met up at REI in Austin. When I pulled up, he was standing beside his super cool black Jeep Wrangler, with lifted tires and a white tent on top. It was the coolest Jeep I'd ever seen. Right away I liked his vibe—he was laid back and so genuine that it caught me off guard in the best way. Immediately, I felt safe around him. When I got in and out of the car, he'd run around the car to open my door. I'd never met such a gentleman before.

I gave myself wiggle room for an easy out if our date didn't go well after hiking, but I was enjoying our time together so much that I didn't want it to end. We decided to grab lunch at a nearby restaurant on Lake Austin. During our lunch, he openly shared his relationship with Jesus, which seemed surprisingly really solid. I could tell Jake was close with Jesus because he carried a natural light that I had only seen in a handful of other men.

The other issue I wanted to investigate was his habits with alcohol. I assumed he was a social drinker since he seemed like a very social guy, so I asked, "Tell me about your relationship with alcohol." I needed to know because I wasn't willing to date a guy who liked to party. I'd been down that road enough and finally learned my lesson.

"Um, I don't really have one. I mean I've tasted a beer before but don't actually like the it, but it's seriously okay if you do," he said with a big smile on his face, taking a sip of his Dr Pepper.

I was genuinely confused. "He must mean he doesn't drink often but when he does, he prefers beer," I said.

He laughed. "No, definitely not, but if you do like beer, that's okay. I don't have a problem with others drinking. Most of my friends drink, so I'll be their designated driver."

I spent the next twenty minutes interrogating him, in disbelief that he never had been drunk before in his life and didn't even like the taste of alcohol. I'd never met someone like this before. I didn't even believe someone like him existed. These were solid confirmations from God: he didn't like the taste of alcohol, he loved Jesus on his own, he was a gentleman, and he made me laugh. In our next few hours together, I felt so relaxed and found myself getting lost in our conversation, I could talk to him for hours. It was so obvious to me that he carried a bright light that was apparent through his genuineness, kindness, confidence, and bold optimism. Jake was in fact my God's best I'd dreamed of.

CONSIDER THIS

"For I know the plans I have for you," says the Lord. "They are plans for good and not for disaster, to give you a future and a hope." (Jer. 29:11)

This verse is a popular one for good reason. It's one that shares God's heart for His children—to give them a future and hope, two things every human is designed to desire.

A big part of my sacrifice and not settling was the time I spent dreaming with God. If I hadn't given Him space and asked Him for a vision of what He wanted for me, then I would have fallen into hopelessness and stayed stuck. I would have believed the childhood lies that I wasn't worthy and that I was too broken. The good news is that God has a plan for you too, in the exact season and age that you are in.

You're not too young, too old, or too sinful—those are all common lies that will keep you stuck in fear and doubt.

Ask the Holy Spirit these three powerful questions:

1. What's Your vision for me five years from now?

2. What's God's heart for me and how does He want to use me in the season I'm currently in?

3. How can I partner with You, Holy Spirit?

Write these down and spend time reviewing them regularly. These are life-changing questions when you spend time answering them with God. It was life changing for me, I still do it on a regular basis, and I plan on doing it till my last days. Give yourself permission to think bigger than what feels possible or comfortable right now. God wants you to dream big because it requires you to trust and rely on Him. In that process, you deepen your faith and learn more about the One for whom nothing is impossible.

I invite you to say this simple prayer:

Heavenly Father, thank You for creating me for a purpose with a future and hope that's better than I can imagine. Thank You for redeeming my steps and that Your grace is sufficient for me. Holy Spirit, help me to hear Your voice more often, so I can listen to where You're calling me. And give me the courage to follow through on where You're leading me. In Jesus's name. Amen.

If you have been running to avoid your heart wounds, feeling nudges that God's calling you to more, but life keeps getting in the way, then I encourage you that saying *yes* to surrendering to Him is better than you can ever imagine. You're never too late! Now, is the perfect time. He loves you. He's calling you to return to Him, fully and completely. Don't wait until you've cleaned up your own messes. Jesus wants to walk hand-in-hand with you through them *all*. **Come home to Him now!**

And if you're waiting for your God's best, like I was, then I encourage you to be sure you're using this time wisely to face insecurities, break bad habits, heal where you need it, and strengthen your faith so you can become the woman or man you want to be for your teammate. The healing work I did and giving up alcohol were two incredible gifts I've been able to give to Jake and our family. You never know who or what God is preparing you for—if you put Him in charge by surrendering, you'll be blown away in the best ways. When you dream with God, the impossible becomes reasonable, no matter what your past looks like. I'm a walking testimony of that.

About the Author

Whit and her husband Jake are co-founders of Steadfast Life Coaching, a faith-based life coaching company, where they help people overcome their obstacles and lies, so they can live more from God's freedom and purpose. They've coached hundreds of people over the last seven years to walk in more freedom, empowerment, and alignment with God's purpose in their life.

They live from the powerful identity of being children of God with an adventure and athlete mindset. They've found that these three identities come from faith-based beliefs that empower them to adventure with God, taking risks and having fun while training each day to be the best athlete: mind, body, and spirit.

If you want more help making changes like these in your life, Jake and Whit have free resources you can access on their website, www.steadfastlifecoaching.com. They use practical tools and faith (based on biblical truths) that have helped Whit transform her mind, body, and spirit to become a walking testimony of God's goodness and grace.

Made in United States
Troutdale, OR
01/27/2024

17233468R00077